Benjamin Hall Kennedy

The Psalter or Psalms of David in English Verse

Benjamin Hall Kennedy

The Psalter or Psalms of David in English Verse

ISBN/EAN: 9783744771764

Printed in Europe, USA, Canada, Australia, Japan

Cover: Foto ©Lupo / pixelio.de

More available books at **www.hansebooks.com**

The Psalter

OR

PSALMS OF DAVID,

IN ENGLISH VERSE.

BY

BENJAMIN HALL KENNEDY, D.D.

CANON OF ELY.

CAMBRIDGE:
DEIGHTON, BELL AND CO.
LONDON: G. BELL AND SONS.
1876.

TO THE

MEMORY OF MY WIFE.

THE TRANSLATOR'S PREFACE.

THE Translator had employed a few of his leisure hours in selecting words for sacred music. He had been thus led to translate Psalms and passages from Psalms, and also to compile and adapt from other translators. The work, as it went on, became a labour of love; the thought of completing and publishing a new version of the Psalter was conceived; and, having obtained the approval of his diocesan and friend, the revered Bishop Lonsdale, he published it (without adding his name) in the year 1860.

In the present Reprint considerable alterations have been made; and the Version (printed but not yet published) of the Old Testament Company of Revisers has been always carefully consulted.

The version is humbly offered as a contribution to the general psalmody of the Christian Church. On this account it has not been deemed requisite to alter every psalm partly borrowed from other sources. But it is a grateful duty to acknowledge the assistance so received.

(1) The Old Version, by Sternhold and Hopkins, has sometimes been followed in a few psalms

of the first book. In Psalm 18, especially, some of its best stanzas will be easily recognized.

(2) George Sandys and another old translator supplied the framework of Psalms 40, 41, 44, 53, 62, 115, 125.

(3) The Rev. Arthur Tozer Russell, with kind liberality, allowed the free use of his published collection of Hymns, which includes a few Psalms and many extracts from Psalms, all much paraphrased for hymnal purpose. Mr Russell's metres have been adopted in the following Psalms: 2, 24, 39, 45, 46, 50, 84, 85, 110, 111, 113; and some of his lines have been retained, though in general it was necessary to bring his rendering nearer to the Hebrew.

(4) Some lines of Psalm 90 are borrowed from Montgomery's version.

All translation from the poetry of one language into that of another must contain some alloy of paraphrase. The present Translator's wish and endeavour has been to adhere as closely as possible to the original Hebrew; but with due regard to perspicuity and poetic expression. In some Psalms (the 87th for instance) he does not see how any version, even in prose, could be at the same time literal and intelligible. But in every place, where he has departed from the literal utterance of the Hebrew, he has tried to follow its general sense and tone. He has given special attention to the use of the sacred names Jah or Jhvh, and Elohim, rendered Lord (sometimes Jehovah) and God. Very seldom (Psalm 29 being a necessary exception) has he omitted either Name where used in the original; more rarely (if ever) has he introduced either, where the sacred writer has not done so.

It has been urged as an argument against poetic versions of the Psalms, that the Hebrew parallelism is a nobler kind of rhythm than any we possess. Be it granted that, as inevitable loss is sustained by rendering the words of inspiration from the original into any other language, so is something lost by exchanging the laws of parallelism for those of metre and rhyme. Yet it will not be denied, that grand truths and thoughts may be conveyed in our rhythms, and that our rhythms become nobler and more useful in proportion as they are the vehicles of such truths and thoughts. And, wedded as the English mind is to the forms in which our great poets have written, there seems no likelihood that English sacred music will ever confine itself to the forms of Hebrew poetry. Some English metrical Psalms (as for instance the Old Hundredth) are so strongly domesticated in our hymnology, that the Christian public would not willingly consent to lose them. Such versions, if true to the meaning of the original, supply valuable help in the spiritual study of the Psalms to ordinary readers ignorant of Hebrew. Psalms 49, 60, 87 may serve to illustrate what is meant: and it may be observed, in passing, that such Psalms as these reasonably admit a more free style of translation than Psalms like 16 and 22, where a closer adherence to the language of the original is eminently desirable. It would seem for these reasons, that improved metrical versions (supposing them truly such) ought not to be unwelcome, as a temporary good, even to those who look for something better than any metrical version. And that translator must be unskilful indeed, who has failed to preserve any of the beauties of Hebrew parallelism, though he could not retain them all.

Conscious of the great difficulty of his task, and of much inevitable imperfection in executing it, the Translator can only hope that this version may not be found in all respects unfit for the purpose of Christian instruction and edification: to which use he prays that God may direct and bless it.

CAMBRIDGE,
Christmas, 1875.

A few corrections are made in this reprint, chiefly suggested by the Translator's kind friends, Canon Perowne and Mr Aldis Wright, to whom his warm thanks are due for the trouble they have taken in comparing this volume with the Hebrew text.

February, 1876.

OBSERVATIONS

ON

THE PSALMS.

———•———

§ 1. THE Psalms are a collection of the sacred and inspired songs of Israel. They are divided according to style and subject into (1) Praise-songs, which thank, bless, and glorify the Lord God: (2) Prayer-songs, which contain supplications and expressions of penitence, grief, pain, alarm, faith, hope, &c.: (3) Instruction-songs, which convey moral and religious doctrines and precepts.

§ 2. The meaning and spirit of the Psalms will be understood by reference to the history and character of the Jewish people, more especially as seen in the Pentateuch, or five books of Moses. They breathe, with all the fervour of lyric feeling, the deep heart of a nation, which believed itself to be under the peculiar rule, guidance, and protection of an Almighty Lord (Jehovah), and this Lord to be the true and only God (Elohim), Creator and Governor of the world. To Him the Psalmists pray for every good they need, in every condition of human life: Him they thank and praise for every good they receive: His dominion they proclaim as supreme: His laws, though given in writing to Israel only, as binding upon all the families of mankind, who shall gradually be received into covenant with Israel and the Lord God of Israel.

§ 3. The Psalms, in number 150, are divided, in imitation of the Pentateuch, into five books, each of which is wound up with a doxology. These books are (1) Psalms 1—41, (2) Psalms 42—72, (3) Psalms 73—89, (4) Psalms 90—106, (5) Psalms 107—150.

§ 4. All the Psalms but thirty-four bear titles or inscriptions, as shown in the English Bible. These titles sometimes name the author: sometimes the character of the Psalm: some contain terms of musical notation, the meaning of which is mere matter of conjecture. Other notations, probably indicating breaks or changes in the music, are interposed between the parts of some Psalms, as the well-known word Selah. The Psalms without titles are: 1, 2, 10, 33, 43, 71, 91, 93, 94, 95, 96, 97, 99, 104, 105, 106, 107, 111, 112, 113, 114, 115, 116, 117, 118, 119, 135, 136, 137, 146, 147, 148, 149, 150. Besides these, sixteen other Psalms are without the writer's name attached. These are: 66, 67, 92, 98, 100, 102, 120, 121, 123, 125, 126, 128, 129, 130, 132, 134. Thus fifty of the Psalms, being one third of the full number, have no author's name inscribed.

§ 5. The titles ascribe the following authorship: (1) Moses: Psalm 90. (2) David: Psalms 3, 4, 5, 6, 7, 8, 9, 11, 12, 13, 14, 15, 16, 17, 18, 19, 20, 21, 22,

23, 24, 25, 26, 27, 28, 29, 30, 31, 32, 34, 35, 36, 37, 38, 39, 40, 41, 51, 52, 53, 54, 55, 56, 57, 58, 59, 60, 61, 62, 63, 64, 65, 68, 69, 70, 86, 101, 103, 108, 109, 110, 122, 124, 131, 133, 138, 139, 140, 141, 142, 143, 144, 145; in all seventy-three. (3) Solomon: Psalms 72 and 127. (4) Asaph, son of Berechiah, a Levite, and David's chief musician, appears as author of twelve Psalms. But of these only seven belong to this Asaph; namely, Psalms 50, 73, 77, 78, 80, 81, 82. The other five, probably written by musical descendants of Asaph, are of later times: Psalm 83, of Jehoshaphat's age; Psalms 75, 76, written in Hezekiah's reign; Psalms 74, 79, during the Captivity of the Jews in Babylon. (5) Eleven Psalms are assigned to the Korahites, a minstrel family descended from the rebel Levite Korah. This family conducted the temple-services as late as the reign of Jehoshaphat (2 Chron. xx. 19). Its head in David's time was Heman (1 Chron. vi. 16; ix. 19). Of these Psalms, 42, 44, 84, are considered to be of the Davidic era; 45, of Solomon's time; 47, 48, of Jehoshaphat's age; 46, 87, of Hezekiah's reign. Psalm 49 has no historical reference: and Psalm 85, though often referred to the Captivity, is by later critics regarded as of earlier, but uncertain, date. Psalm 88 is ascribed in the title both to the Korahites, and to Heman the Ezrahite: whence it is supposed that this Heman obtained incorporation into the tribe of Levi and family of Korah. (6) Psalm 89 is attributed to Ethan the Ezrahite, who is one with Jeduthun, David's choir-master.

§ 6. Among the fifty anonymous Psalms, 1, 2, 10, 33, are very probably compositions of David himself; 43, a Korahite Psalm of the Davidic age; 66, of Hezekiah's time; 71, 91, 92, 93, 94, 95, 96, 97, 98, 99, 100, of various dates between Solomon's reign and the Captivity : 102 (perhaps also 104, 105 and 106) during the Captivity; 67, indeterminate: the remainder (see § 4) by unknown authors in various years after the return of the Jews from Captivity; the four concluding Psalms being probably written for the dedication of the city-walls by Nehemiah. There is however much uncertainty as to the dates of some Psalms. Hengstenberg assigns Psalms 66, 67, 71, 102, to David, and Psalm 86 not to David, but to a Korahite of his suite: thus making the Davidic Psalms exactly eighty in number.

§ 7. The Psalms, as they stand in the Sacred Canon, are obviously arranged on an artificial principle, according to their subject-matter. This proves that the collection was formed at one time and by one person; as some suppose, by Ezra; but more probably by an unknown editor during the government of Nehemiah. At the head of the Psalms, by way of preface, stands the description of the truly righteous, who is also the truly happy, man (Psalm 1), probably selected from the then extant works of David. Then follow in three books various Psalms of David and his contemporaries, the founders and masters of Hebrew Psalmody. It has been observed that the general arrangement of these Psalms depends on the name assigned in them to the Supreme Being. Jehovah-Psalms are those in which the name exclusively or chiefly used is Jehovah (which we render 'the Lord'), His peculiar title as the God of Israel : while Elohim-Psalms are those in which He bears, wholly or chiefly, the more universal title of Elohim, the God of creation and providence. In the first book are contained the Jehovah-Psalms of David ; in the second, the Elohim-Psalms of the Korahites, Asaph, David himself, Solomon, &c. ; in the third, the remaining Korahite and Asaphite Psalms, which are partly Jehovah-Psalms, partly mixed (Jehovah-Elohim-Psalms): and, within the several books, those Psalms are evidently brought together which have some common bond, either of subject, style, or title. In the two latter books a general chronological arrangement prevails. They begin with the Song of Moses (Psalm 90), which is followed by ten Psalms of the times before the Captivity, and these again by six Psalms, of which two at least are taken from the works of David (101, 103,) while the remaining four may be of the Babylonian era. In the last book, it is very likely that Psalm 107 was written for the first celebration of the Feast of Tabernacles after the return from exile : next follow three Psalms from the Davidic collection : then nine others (111—119) which may have been sung on laying the foundations of the new temple; Psalm 119 being in the nature of a sermon for the young at the close. Psalms 113—118 were afterwards called the great Hallel, and were sung at all the Jewish feasts, especially at the Passover and the feast of Tabernacles (Math. xxvi. 30). Psalms 120—134 are called 'Songs of degrees,' and form 'the pilgrim's little book.' They are supposed to be so called from being sung, severally, on the fifteen steps in the sanctuary between the men's and women's court, when the pilgrim Jews came to the yearly feasts. They comprise four Psalms of David, one of Solomon, and ten anonymous. The next group of twelve Psalms, 135—146, was sung after the completion of the temple, and probably at its consecration. It begins with three nameless Psalms and ends with another nameless one, the remaining eight being taken from the works of David. The last four Psalms are nameless, and, as before mentioned, they were probably sung at the dedication of the city-walls under Nehemiah.

§ 8. Hence it appears on what just grounds rests the title usually given to the Psalter, 'The Psalms of David.' Not only was that illustrious prince and poet the composer of about half the entire collection, or, if we add his musicians, of above three-fifths, but with every book are incorporated some of his Psalms, to give as it were the key-note, the tone and character, to the rest. Furthermore, although lyric poetry existed in Israel at an earlier period (Numb. xxi. 14; Josh. x. 13), and psalmody revived under Samuel in the schools of the prophets (1 Sam. x. 5), yet its full bloom and development were reserved for the reign of 'the sweet singer of Israel.' For the public performance of psalms David instituted a sacred choir of singers, standing himself at its head: after him came Asaph, Heman, Jeduthun; then their twenty-four sons, namely, four sons of Asaph, six of Jeduthun, fourteen of Heman: and of these sons each had a class of twelve singers under him, formed of their kindred. Four thousand Levites were also set apart for the musical services. Asaph and his company were placed on mount Zion, with the ark of the covenant (all these arrangements dating from its instalment there), and Heman and Jeduthun with the holy tent at Gibeon (1 Chron. xvi. 37). For other details and for the history of psalmodic poetry and music from the days of David to those of Nehemiah, consult Hengstenberg's Appendix to his Commentary on the Psalms. See also the commentaries of Hupfeld, Delitzsch, Prof. Perowne; and that of Canon Cook in the Speaker's Commentary.

§ 9. After setting aside the Song of Moses, Psalm 90 (B. C. 1500), we find about three-fifths of the whole Psalter ascribable to the reign of David, including the few last years of Saul, and the first of Solomon (B. C. 1060—1000). We have then a few Psalms of Jehoshaphat's reign (B. C. 914—889): while of the rest some belong to the times of the Assyrian and Chaldean devastations (B. C. 740—588), some to the Captivity (B.C. 588—536), many others to the period between the restoration of the Jews and the dedication of the city-walls (B. C. 536—445).

§ 10. The Psalms may be viewed, in general, as inspired delineations of spiritual religion. The other sacred books teach us how to think and act: this teaches us also how to feel. Here is shown the immortal soul stirred by the manifold emotions and affections to which it is subject through the sanctifying influences of the Holy Spirit. Here we see it variously moved in various circumstances. We see it in its hopes and fears, in its joys and sorrows, in its exultation and depression; in its confessions, prayers, and praises; in its faith, resignation, patience and humility; in the severity of conflict, and in the triumph of victory; in the trembling of despondence and in the vigour of confidence; in the day of cloud and darkness, and in the season when the storm is hushed, the sun bright, and the prospect clear and extended. Hence it has been well said, that 'the Psalms are as it were the anatomy of a holy man, which lay the inside of a truly devout man outward to the view of others. If the Scriptures be compared to a body, the Psalms may well be the heart, they are so full of sweet affections and passions. For in other portions of Scripture God speaks to us; but in the Psalms holy men speak to God and to their own hearts.'—(SIBBES.)

§ 11. But the crowning glory of the Psalms is the witness which they bear, by type and prophecy, to the divine Saviour of the world. This Messiah had been promised to Adam first, then to Abraham: Israel was separated for the purpose of blessing all mankind, and out of the tribe of Judah (so said the dying Jacob in the Spirit) was to arise the Shiloh, the Restorer of all nations. This prophecy is linked on to the Psalms by the promise conveyed through Nathan (2 Sam. vii. 12—17), which settled great hopes on David and his family. But, in addition to this promise, fulfilled first in Solomon, afterwards in the Lord Jesus Christ the Son of David, we find in David himself a great prophet and type of Christ. Foreshown in the prophetic Psalms (most of which are David's) we see many of the most important features of Messiah and His reign. A king is set upon the holy hill of Zion; he is opposed by the kings of the earth, whose rage is defeated (Psalm 2); we read of his sceptre of righteousness and divine sonship (Psalm 45); his unchangeable priesthood and all-conquering sway (Psalm 110); his sufferings (Psalm 22), and resurrection, escaping the corruption of the grave (Psalm 16); his ascension to a throne of glory (Psalm 24); his dominion embracing both Israel and the Gentile world (Psalms 2, 22, 33, 67, 72, 89, 132, 138, &c.). All these are shown in passages prophetic of Christ and His kingdom: while, at the same time, David, in most of his own Psalms, and in those of other writers, is himself a conspicuous type of his divine Son in the flesh, as King, as Prophet, as Conqueror, as Sufferer, as obedient in each character to the will of God, in whom he puts his trust. Thus the Psalms are full of Christ; and, as Israel, Jerusalem, and Mount Zion, the holy nation, city, and sanctuary, are types of Christ's Church, we have in the Psalms a book of inspiration which the Christian may justly apply to his own manifold interests in relation to God and Christ, to this world and the world to come. It is obvious, (says Bishop Horne), that every part of the Psalter, when explicated according to this scriptural and primitive method, is rendered universally 'profitable for doctrine, for reproof, for correction, for instruction in righteousness;' and the propriety immediately appears of its having always been used, in the devotional way, both by the Jewish and the Christian Church. With regard to the Jews, Bishop Chandler very pertinently remarks that 'they must have understood David their prince to have been a figure of Messiah. They would not otherwise have made his Psalms part of their daily worship, nor would David have delivered them to the Church to be so employed, were it not to instruct and support them in the knowledge and belief of his fundamental article. Was the Messias not concerned in the Psalms, it were absurd to celebrate, twice a day in their public devotions, the events of one man's life, who was deceased so long ago as to have no relations of their affairs, or to transcribe whole passages from them in their prayers for the coming of the Messiah.' Upon the same principle, it is easily seen that the objections which may seem to lie against the use of Jewish services in Christian congregations cease at once. Thus, it may be said, Are we concerned with the affairs of David and of Israel? Have we anything to do with the ark and the temple? They are no more. Are we to go up to Jerusalem, and to worship on Zion? They are desolated and trodden under foot by the Turks. Are we to sacrifice young bullocks according to the law? The law is abolished, never to be observed again. Do we pray for victory over Moab, Edom and Philistia? or for deliverance from Babylon? There are no such nations, no such places in the world. What then do we mean, when, taking such expressions into our mouths, we utter them in our own persons, as part of our devotions, before God? Assuredly we must mean a spiritual Jerusalem and Zion; a spiritual ark and temple; a spiritual law; spiritual sacrifices, and spiritual victories over spiritual enemies; all described under the old names, which are still retained, though 'old things are passed away, and all things are become new.' By substituting Messiah for David, the gospel for the law, the Church Christian for that of Israel, and the enemies of the one for those of the other, the Psalms are made our own. Nay, they are with more fulness and propriety applied now to the substance, than they were of old to the 'shadow of good things then to come.'

§ 12. These things being considered, we cannot wonder that in all ages of the Church the saints of God should have found in the Psalms a rich storehouse of comfort and delight, instruction and devotion. Volumes might be filled with the overflowings of their grateful affection for this divine Book. Enough here to cite the testimonies of three holy members of the one Holy Catholic Church,—the first belonging to its Oriental, the second to its African, the last to its Anglican branch.

'All scripture,' says St Basil, 'divinely inspired and profitable, was for this purpose written of the Spirit, that, as in a common medicine-shop of souls, every man might select the medicine fit for his peculiar disease. For, indeed, some things the Prophets teach us, others the Historians, others the Law, others the Proverbs. But this one Book of Psalms comprehends in itself what is profitable in all. It foretells things to come; it records histories; it gives laws for life; it prescribes what things should be done; in a word, it is a common store-house of good doctrines, bringing to every one things found out for his use with singular care.' (*Homil. in Ps.* 1.)

'What is there,' says St Augustine, 'which may not be learnt in the Psalms? Have we not proceeding from them the greatness of all virtue, the rule of justice, the comeliness of purity, the perfection of prudence, the pattern of patience, every good, in short, which can be named? The knowledge of God, the full prediction of Christ to come in the flesh, the hope of a common resurrection, the fear of punishment, the promise of glory, the revelation of mysteries, yea, all good things are hid and heaped together in these Psalms as in some great and public treasury.' (*Prolog. in Psalm.*)

'The choice and flower of all things profitable in other books,' says saintly Hooker, 'the Psalms doth more briefly contain, and more movingly also express, by reason of that poetic form wherewith they are written. The ancients, when they speak of the book of Psalms, use to fall into large discourses, showing how this part above the rest doth of purpose set forth and celebrate all the considerations and operations which belong to God; it magnifieth the holy meditations and actions of divine men; it is of things heavenly a universal declaration, working in them, whose heart God inspireth with the due consideration thereof, a habit or disposition of mind whereby they are made fit vessels for receipt and for delivery of whatsoever perfection. What is there necessary for man to know, which the Psalms are not able to teach? They are to beginners an easy and familiar introduction; a mighty augmentation of all virtue and knowledge in such as are entered before; a strong confirmation to the most perfect among others. Heroical magnanimity, exquisite justice, grave moderation, exact wisdom, repentance unfeigned, unwearied patience, the mysteries of God, the sufferings of Christ, the terrors of wrath, the comforts of grace, the works of providence over this world, and the promised joys of the world which is to come; all good to be necessarily either known, or done, or had, this one celestial fountain yieldeth. Let there be any grief or disease incident unto the soul of man, any wound or sickness named, for which there is not, in this treasure-house, a present comfortable remedy at all times ready to be found. Hereof it is that we covet to make the Psalms especially familiar unto all.' (*Eccles. Pol.* v. 37.)

THE PSALMS OF DAVID.

PSALM I.

How blest the man, who fears to stray
  Where godless people meet,
Nor stands with sinners in the way,
  Nor fills the scorner's seat:

But finding in the Lord's pure law
  A well-spring of delight,
He ponders it with holy awe
  Devoutly day and night.

As some fair tree, which has its root
  The flowing waters nigh,
Brings forth its seasonable fruit
  And leaves that never die,

Thus all he doeth prospers well:
  Not so the wicked fare:
Like driven chaff when breezes swell,
  They waver here and there.

Hence, in the day when hearts are tried,
  The godless shall not stand;
Nor may the sinner then abide
  Among the righteous band,

The Lord's just eyes behold and bless
　　The good man's daily path;
But every way of wickedness
　　Shall perish in His wrath.

PSALM II.

Why do the heathen rage?
　　What are the nations dreaming?
In vain against the Lord
　　And His Anointed scheming,
Kings of the earth arise,
　　And leaguèd princes say:
'Come, let us break their bands, and cast
　　Their cords from us away.'

He who is throned in heaven
　　Derides their preparation;
The Lord upon them pours
　　His scornful indignation:
Soon shall His voice of wrath
　　Their souls with anguish thrill:
'Yet have I set My King upon
　　My Zion's holy hill.'—

Now will I cry aloud
　　And tell the Lord's great token:
'Thou art My Son,' He saith:
　　To Me the word was spoken:
'Yea, Thee have I this day
　　Begotten: ask of Me,
Thy heritage the heathen, Thine
　　Earth's utmost parts shall be:

Beneath Thine iron rod
  Thy foemen shall be shattered,
As by the potter's hand
  The broken sherds are scattered.'
Be wise, then, O ye kings,
  Ye earthly judges, hear;
Serve ye the Lord with trembling awe,
  Rejoice with wholesome fear.

Bow down and kiss the Son,
  Lest, if His wrath awaken,
Ye perish in the way,
  For evermore forsaken:
Let but His anger rise,
  Though little be the flame—
How blessèd above all are they
  That trust His holy Name!

PSALM III.

O Lord, how great the adverse host!
  How many rage around!
'No rescue for his soul,' they boast,
  'No help in God is found.'

But Thou my head exaltest high,
  My shield, my glory still;
The Lord gave answer to my cry
  From out His holy hill.

I laid me down in calm repose;
  I slept, from peril free;
In peace I slept, in strength arose,
  The Lord sustaineth me.

Though myriad foes beset my road,
  No fear my heart shall know;
Arise, O Lord; help, O my God:
  Thou smitest every foe;

With riven jaws and broken teeth
  My godless haters flee :
Lord, on Thine own a blessing breathe :
  Salvation comes from Thee.

PSALM IV.

GOD of my righteousness,
  To Thee I cry; give ear :
Thou Saviour in my past distress,
  Be merciful and hear.

O sons of men, my right
  How long will ye despise?
In emptiness how long delight,
  And follow after lies?

But know, the faithful heart
  Unto the Lord is dear:
He sets it for Himself apart :
  My prayer the Lord will hear.

Abide in holy dread,
  And cease from doing ill:
With your own heart upon your bed
  Hold converse, and be still.

Your just oblation bring,
  A mind without offence,
And to the Lord's protection cling
  With pious confidence.

Many there be that cry,
  'Who now will show us grace?'—
Lift on us, Lord, Thy loving eye,
  The glory of Thy face.

A joy from Thee more bright
  Within my heart will shine
Than theirs who view with deep delight
  Their plenteous corn and wine.

With peaceful trust in Thee,
  I lay me down and sleep;
For safely, Lord, though lone I be,
  My dwelling Thou wilt keep.

PSALM V.

GIVE ear unto my words, O Lord,
  Regard my lowly sighs:
Hear, O my King, my God; to Thee
  I come with earnest cries.

Receive, O Lord, my morning voice;
  To Thee at break of day
My prayer I order, looking forth
  To find Thee, when I pray.

No God that loveth ill art Thou;
  No mischief dwells with Thee:
Thine eyes reject the proud, and such
  As work iniquity.

With ruin dire on lying lips
  Thy shafts of vengeance fall:
Bloodthirsty and deceitful men,
  The Lord abhors them all.

But I unto Thy house will come
  In Thine abundant grace,
And in the fear of Thee bow down
  Before Thy holy place.

O lead me by Thy righteousness;
  The way that I should go
Make plain, O Lord, before my face;
  For near me lurks the foe.

No stedfast word is in their mouth;
  Their thoughts are guile and wrong;
Their throat an open sepulchre;
  They flatter with their tongue.

O God, condemn them: let their craft
  Their own o'erthrowing be;
And in their height of sin destroy
  The rebels against Thee.

But glad be they whose trust Thou art;
  Thanksgivings they shall sing
To Thee for evermore, who rest
  Beneath Thy guardian wing.

Who love Thy Name in Thee rejoice;
  For to the just is sealed
Thy blessing, Lord; Thy sheltering grace
  Defends them like a shield.

PSALM VI.

LORD, in Thy wrath rebuke me not,
  Nor in Thy withering ire chastise;
O spare and heal: my bones are hot,
  My troubled heart within me dies.

But Thou, O Lord, how long?—Set free
  My soul, and in Thy mercy save:
For none in death remembers Thee;
  What tongue shall praise Thee in the grave?

Weary of sighing I am grown,
  And, sick with daily griefs and fears,
At night I lay me weeping down,
  And water all my couch with tears.

Though, dim with sorrow, fades mine eye,
  And shrunk with terror of the foe;
Fly, ye who work injustice, fly;
  The Lord hath heard my voice of woe:

The Lord hath heard, and in His grace
  He gives my praying heart repose;
But shuddering dread and shame of face
  And headlong flight, await my foes.

PSALM VII.

O LORD my God, I seek in Thee
  My refuge and repose:
Save Thou my life, and rescue me
  From persecuting foes:

Lest, lion-like, his ruthless hate
  My soul in pieces rend,
And none be present in my strait
  To succour and defend.

O Lord my God, if I have dared
  This wicked deed to do,
To harm the peaceful (I who spared
  Erewhile a causeless foe),

Then let the fierce pursuer's might
  My fainting soul inthral,
Tread down my life, my glory blight,
  And triumph in my fall.

Rise in Thy wrath, O Lord: appear
  Against the foeman's pride:
Awake, and let the people hear
  Thy sentence on my side.

Yea, throned above the listening throng
  Give judgment, Lord, for me,
As I have shunned the path of wrong
  And kept integrity.

O quell the baneful power of sin,
  And make the just secure:
Thou triest the heart and reins within,
  A righteous God and pure.

God is my shield; with saving rod
  He keeps His servant's way;
God is an upright judge, a God
  Who chastens day by day.

And turn we not? He whets His sword,
  His bow is bent in ire,
His instruments of death are stored,
  His arrows tipt with fire,

To strike the man who travails long
  With dark iniquity,
Conceiving only guile and wrong,
  And bringing forth a lie.

He digged and delved a pit, and lo,
  His feet are in the toils;
On his own head returns the woe,
  On him his rage recoils.

For all His goodness I will bless
  The Lord, who heard my cry,
And with a song of praise confess
  His Name, the Lord Most High.

PSALM VIII.

O LORD our Lord, how bright thy fame
In all the earth, how great Thy Name,
Thou who hast made the heavenly height
The dwelling of Thy glorious light!

Thy strength in weakness oft is shown;
Thy power when babes and sucklings own,
The angry foe their mouths control,
And still the fierce avenger's soul.

Oft do I muse, with reverent eyes
Reading the beauty of the skies,
The moon and stars, that ordered stand
Obedient to Thy framing hand:

'O what is man, that in Thy mind
His works and ways remembrance find?
Or what the child of man, to share
Thy fostering love, Thy guardian care?

Next to the angel host in place
He stands, the nursling of Thy grace,
An heir of heaven, a son of light,
With worship crowned, with glory bright:

He stands, Thy chosen deputy,
To rule the creatures formed by Thee:
Thy power beneath his feet has laid
Whate'er on earth that power has made.

To man's dominion all must yield,
The sheep and oxen of the field,
The wild beast in his forest lair,
The wild bird sailing through the air,

The fishes that in ocean glide,
And myriad nations of the tide.
O Lord our Lord, how bright Thy fame
In all the earth, how great Thy Name!'

PSALM IX. Part I.

ALL my heart shall bless Thee, Lord,
   And Thy wondrous works proclaim;
All my joy shall be Thy Word,
   And my song Thy glorious Name:
From whose face my foemen fly
Falling, fading, Lord Most High.

Holy Judge, be praise to Thee:
   Seated on Thy dreadful throne
Thou hast owned my righteous plea;
   Thou hast cast the nations down:
And the reign of sin is o'er,
Blotted out for evermore.

From the book of life effaced
   All the foes their doom have found;
Laid by Thee for ever waste,
   And uprooted from the ground,
Sink the cities of their pride:
Yea, their very fame hath died.

But for ever sits the Lord,
　　Judging earth with holy laws;
And His firmly-stablished Word
　　Tries aright the people's cause:
He the refuge, He the tower
Of the poor in trouble's hour.

All to whom Thy Name is known
　　Thee their guide and guardian make;
Souls that seek Thy grace alone,
　　Lord, Thou never wilt forsake.
Praise the Lord, declare His might,
His, who dwells on Zion's height.

Part II.

The righteous Lord at tyrant' hands
The poor man's guiltless blood demands;
And ever with regardful ear
From heaven his just complaint will hear.

Whilst angry men my steps pursue,
Thy servant's woes in mercy view,
O Lord, whose love sustains my breath,
And lifts me from the gates of death.

So shall Thy praise my tongue employ,
And Zion's portals hear my joy,
When there with thankful heart I sing
The strong salvation of her King.

The heathen in the pit are laid
Their craftiness for others made,
And start with sudden awe, to find
In their own net their feet entwined.

His judgments thus the Lord displays,
And mischief with itself repays:
Hell is the sinner's bourne, in hell
The God-forgetting nations dwell.

For dream not that without a friend
The poor shall languish to the end;
That lost in drear oblivion's shade
The mourner's hopes for ever fade.

Rise, Lord, and let not man presume;
On heathen scorners speak Thy doom:
For they shall crouch in terror then,
And know themselves to be but men.

PSALM X. PART I.

WHY seems it good to Thee, O Lord,
   So far aloof to stand?
Why hidest Thou Thy face away,
   When trouble is at hand?

The scorner's pride pursues the poor,
   And hunts their harmless lives;
May he be taken in the net
   His cunning guile contrives.

For in the lusts of his own heart
   The wicked finds delight;
The covetous against the Lord
   Pours out his boastful spite.

The providence that rules on high
   His daring thoughts despise:
'There is no God above,' he says,
   'No all-observing eyes.'

Strong in his sinful path, he sets
  Thy judgments, Lord, aside:
His enemies he puffs away
  With scornful blasts of pride.

'Tush, tush,' he cries, 'no change I dread;
  I bear a charmèd lot;
To me and mine from age to age
  Ill fortune cometh not.'

Within his mouth a curse is found,
  Upon his lips a lie,
Beneath his tongue deceit and guile
  And foul iniquity.

Behind the villages he prowls
  To slay the innocent:
Upon the poor who pass him by
  His lawless eyes are bent:

E'en as a lion privily
  Lies lurking in his den,
So in his ambush lurks the proud
  To ravage helpless men:

He boweth down, he croucheth low,
  To snare and seize his prey;
And God, he thinks, will never see,
  God hides His face away.

Part II.

O Lord, arise; lift up Thine hand,
O God, and heal the sorrowing land:
Arise to save the meek: for why
Should impious tongues our God defy?

They mutter in their secret mind:
'God will not judge us; God is blind.'
But Thou hast seen: all wicked ways
Lie open to Thy piercing gaze.

Recorded by Thy righteous hand
The sinner's deeds for judgment stand:
To Thee the poor commits his cause,
His help from Thee the orphan draws:

Break Thou the wicked arm, and beat
The proud oppressor from his seat:
Proclaim—The reign of sin is o'er,
The place that knew it knows no more.

O Lord the King of endless might,
The heathen perish from Thy sight:
'Tis Thine the drooping heart to cheer,
The cries of praying saints to hear,

The orphan's injured cause to try,
And, in Thy people's peril nigh,
To snatch them from the spoiler's rage,
And guard their rightful heritage.

PSALM XI.

My refuge is the Lord Most High:
Why hears my soul the faithless cry,
'Ye birds, unto your mountain fly:

For lo, the scorner's bow is bent,
His shaft is on the string, intent
To slay unseen the innocent:

The columns all are out of place,
O'erthrown, uprooted from their base:
What shall they do, the righteous race?'

The Lord is in His temple shrined,
The Lord in heaven; He is not blind;
His eyes behold and judge mankind.

The Lord makes trial of the good;
His soul abhors the ungodly brood,
The hands of violence and blood:

On these His snares shall fall amain,
His sulphurous blast, His fiery rain:
Such cup shall be for them to drain.

The righteous Lord regards with love
The righteous seed: where'er they rove,
They see His guiding face above.

PSALM XII.

SAVE me, O Lord; the good decay;
  The faithful from the world depart;
The liar rules with subtle sway,
  The glozing lip, the double heart.

The flatterer's guile the Lord shall quell,
  The mouth that speaks with boastful glee:
'Our tongues in matchless power excel,
  Our lips are ours; what lord have we?'

He hears the needy's painful sighs,
  He sees the hearts that inly mourn,
And 'Lo, I come,' He saith, 'I rise
  To save thee from the proud man's scorn.'

Thy Word is pure and perfect, Lord,
  As silver in the furnace tried:
Seven times assayed, that holy Word
  Seven times hath come forth purified.

The souls, O Lord, that with Thee walk
  Thy love will shield in evil hour,
On every side though sinners stalk,
  And vileness climbs to lofty power.

PSALM XIII.

How long forgotten, Lord, by Thee,
Forbidden still Thy face to see,
Shall I, by daily grief distrest,
Take counsel with my doubtful breast?

How long amidst triumphant foes,
Who mock my agonizing woes,
To heaven's high throne must I complain,
And seek the Lord my God in vain?

Consider, Lord, and hear my cries,
Pour light upon my darkling eyes,
Lest, yielding up my weary breath,
I sleep the dreamless sleep of death;

Lest o'er my fall the foe rejoice,
And cry with loud exulting voice:
'Lo where he lies, a trampled clod,
Who vainly trusted in his God.'

But I will ever trust Thee, Lord;
My joy is in Thy saving Word:
Thy bounteous mercies I will bless,
And sing of all Thy tenderness.

PSALM XIV.

'There is no God' the fool hath said
　In his vain heart alone :
Corrupt are they : their acts are vile :
　None doeth good, not one.

The Lord looked down from heaven upon
　The children of mankind,
Yet saw He none that wisely sought
　The living God to find :

Astray they went ; a seed perverse,
　In hateful ways they ran ;
Not any good was in the world,
　Nor any godly man.

'Have they no knowledge, evil works
　Who work with one accord,
And eat My people e'en as bread,
　Nor call upon the Lord ?'

But lo ! they tremble : on their hearts
　A sudden horror fell :
For God among the saints of earth
　Abides and loves them well.

Upon the counsels of the poor
　Ye cast reproach and shame ;
Because their refuge is the Lord,
　Their trust His mighty Name.

But what salvation springs for us
　From Zion's holy height ?
And when to Israel will the Lord
　Return with healing light ?

When He shall bring His people home,
   And break their captive chain,
The face of Jacob shall rejoice,
   And Israel smile again.

PSALM XV.

WITHIN Thy tabernacle, Lord,
   Who comes a welcome guest?
Or who upon Thy holy hill
   Shall find his endless rest?

The man whose walk is incorrupt,
   Whose deeds are pure and right,
Whose heart intends the very truth,
   And knows no cunning sleight:

He bears no slander on his lips,
   Nor works a brother wrong,
Nor stabs a neighbour's honest fame
   With evil-speaking tongue:

His stedfast mind is ever set
   The godless to contemn,
But hearts that truly fear the Lord,
   He maketh much of them:

He to his own hurt keeps his oath,
   His gold hath never lent
To grinding use, nor taken bribes
   Against the innocent.

Who thus hath kept Thy perfect law,
   Shall never quit Thy rest,
But on Thy holy hill abide
   An everlasting guest.

PSALM XVI.

Save me, O God; for Thou alone
  My trusted refuge art;
'Thou art my Lord, my only good';
  I spake it from my heart.

And of the saints who dwell on earth,
  The men of perfect mind,
I said, 'With these alone I walk,
  In these my pleasure find.'

But they who seek another God
  Great sorrow find and shame:
I loathe their idol-gifts of blood,
  My lips abhor their name.

The Lord alone supplies my cup,
  My rich inheritance;
And Thou art He that guards my lot
  From every evil chance.

The fields wherein my lines are cast
  In loveliness excel,
And in her pleasant heritage
  My soul delights to dwell.

I thank the Lord who teaches me
  To read His will aright;
Yea, by His blessing do my reins
  Correct me every night.

The Lord I place before my face
  And trust in Him alone:
At my right hand the Lord doth stand;
  I shall not be o'erthrown.

Therefore my heart is very glad;
  My glory shall rejoice;
My flesh in tranquil hope shall rest;
  For Thou wilt crown Thy choice:

Thou wilt not leave my soul in hell,
  So dear it is to Thee;
Nor wilt Thou yield Thy Holy One
  Corruption's doom to see.

Thou showest me the path of life:
  Thy presence hath in store
Fulness of joy; at Thy right hand
  Are pleasures evermore.

PSALM XVII.

Unto my rightful words, O Lord,
  Thy gracious ear incline;
Attend and hearken to my prayer:
  No feignèd lips are mine.

O may the judgment of my cause
  Proceed from only Thee;
Yea, open Thou Thy searching eyes,
  And look on equity.

Thy nightly visitings have tried
  And proved my heart within,
But found no guile: I sware and said
  'My mouth shall never sin'.

From all the works of godless men,
  And ways perverse and ill,
For love of Thy most holy Name
  I have withdrawn me still.

Hold up my goings in Thy paths,
  Nor let my footsteps slide:
To Thee, who answerest prayer, O God,
  My soul hath ever cried.

And yet again I call on Thee,
  For Thou wilt yet reply:
Incline Thine ear unto my speech,
  And hearken to my cry.

Saviour of those that seek Thy face,
  Thy wondrous kindness show,
The prowess of Thy strong right hand
  Against the rampant foe.

O guard me still, as they that guard
  The apple of an eye,
And under covert of Thy wings
  Defend me secretly,

Safe from the wicked seed, whose thoughts
  Are all intent on strife,
Safe from the bitter enemies
  Who rage against my life.

Their dull unfeeling hearts are closed,
  Their mouths defiance sound;
They prowl about our steps, and watch
  To strike us to the ground,

Like ravening lion, or the beast
  That lurketh by the way:—
Rise, Lord, prevent him with Thy sword,
  The cruel slayer slay.

Preserve me by Thy hand, O Lord,
  From men whose lap runs o'er
With earthly good, whose thankless hearts
  Thou satest from Thy store:

Large spoil they leave to lusty sons;
  But I shall see Thy face
In righteousness, and wake to bless
  The fulness of Thy grace.

PSALM XVIII.

How truly do I love Thee, Lord,
  My strength, my confidence:
The Lord is near in peril's hour,
  My castle of defence,

My God, the rock in whom I trust,
  The worker of my wealth,
My lofty stronghold and my shield,
  The horn of all my health.

Oft as I call upon His Name,
  Alone to be adored,
He hastes to save, and all my foes
  Are scattered by the Lord.

The toils of death encompassed me,
  And filled my heart with dread,
The angry waves of wickedness
  Were flowing o'er my head:

The sly and subtle cords of hell
  Were round about me set,
And for my soul there was prepared
  A deadly snaring net.

With pain and grief thus sore bestead,
  I prayed to God for grace,
And He in mercy heard my plaint
  From out His holy place:

He heard my cry, and in His wrath
  He made the earth to shake,
The deep foundations of the hills
  To totter and to quake:

Forth from His nostril came the smoke
  Of His enkindled ire,
Forth from His mouth the lighted coals
  Of hot consuming fire.

The Lord descended from above
  And bowed the heavens on high,
And underneath His feet He cast
  The darkness of the sky:

On cherub pinions charioted
  Full royally He rode,
And on the wings of mighty winds
  Came flying all abroad.

As in the shadow of a den
  He chose His secret place,
With waters black and pilèd clouds
  He canopied His face:

But when His beaming countenance
  Far round its brightness spread,
Clouds were no more, but coals of fire
  And hailstones in their stead.

Thundered the Lord, and in the heaven
  The voice of the Most High
Midst hail and fiery flames was heard;
  His hurtling arrows fly;

Among the foes His lightnings fall,
  And heaving with the shock
Bare lies the bed of ocean, bare
  The world's sustaining rock.

Mid the wild uproar sent the Lord
  To raise me from below,
To pluck me out of waters vast,
  That would my soul o'erflow.

Strong were my foes; against my life
  Their hatred fiercely strove;
But stronger in my day of need
  The Lord's protecting love.

He brought me to an open place,
  From fear and peril free,
And kept me safe: the Lord my God
  Such favour had to me.

According to my truth, I found
  The kindness of the Lord,
According as my hands were clean
  I reaped a rich reward.

Because I chose to keep His ways,
  Nor from my God depart,
Because His judgments and His laws
  I held with faithful heart,

Because I fled the paths of sin,
  The Lord requited me
According to mine innocence
  And mine integrity.

Thou showest, Lord, unto the good
  The goodness of Thy grace,
And to the pure and perfect man
  Thy pure and perfect face:

While from the saints who love Thee well
  Thy love will never swerve,
Thou dealest with the froward seed
  As froward hearts deserve:

Thou liftest up the simple folk
  When they in trouble lie;
But arrogance Thou bringest down,
  Proud soul and haughty eye.

Thy hand it is that lights my lamp,
  And it shall glisten bright;
The Lord my God is He who makes
  My darkness to be light.

Be Thou my strength, an host of men
  Before my arm shall fall;
Be God my help, I shall o'erleap
  The high embattled wall.

The way of God is undefiled,
  His word is purely tried,
He is a buckler sure to all
  Who in His faith abide.

For who is God beside the Lord?
   In heaven and earth is none;
Or who a rock invincible
   Except our God alone?

The God who girdeth me with might,
   Who makes my pathway clear,
And on my valiant feet bestows
   The swiftness of the deer,

He plants me on the castled steep;
   To battle with the foe
He trains my hand; He nerves my arm
   To bend a brazen bow.

Thy cheering grace is nigh to shield,
   Thy right hand to sustain;
Thy gentle chastening casts me down
   To raise me high again.

By Thee I tread an open field
   With firm unfaltering foot,
Nor, till the o'ertaken foemen die,
   Forsake the swift pursuit.

I smite, beneath my feet they fall;
   For the strong battle-blow
Thou giv'st me power: Thy succour lays
   My bold gainsayers low.

My scorners fly before Thy face;
   Who hate my name, I slay:
They cry, but there is none to save,
   No answer when they pray.

I beat them small, as driving winds
  The dust; beneath my feet
I trample them as trodden mire
  Within a crowded street.

By Thee the heathen tribes are tamed
  And me their ruler own:
A people whom I never knew
  Bows down before my throne:

The stranger fawns on my renown,
  And, shrinking from the field
With daunted heart, the aliens haste
  Their mountain forts to yield.

Praised be my rock, the living Lord,
  And blest be God, my tower,
God, mine avenger, who subdues
  The nations to my power:

He saves me from my foes; o'er all
  Who rise against my life
He lifts me high; He rescues me
  From every son of strife.

So will I praise Thee, Lord, Thy Name
  Among the nations sing,
Who guardest David and his seed,
  Thy own anointed king.

PSALM XIX.

THE heavens, O God, Thy glory tell,
  Thy skill the starry firmament;
Day unto day repeats the spell,
  And night to night is eloquent:

No language anywhere, no speech
But thither do their voices reach.

To all the earth their lessons run,
   To utmost shores their herald cry:
A tent amidst them for the sun
   The hand divine hath set on high:
As bridegroom from his chamber, he
Comes forth arrayed in brilliancy:

Like warrior rushing to the fray,
   He glories in his path of light:
From heaven's first gate he takes his way,
   To heaven's far goal he wings his flight:
No spot in universal space
But glows beneath his ardent face.

Sweet is Thy soul-restoring Word,
   Thy law, which makes the simple wise,
Heart-soothing are Thy statutes, Lord,
   Thy truth is light unto the eyes;
Thy fear abides for ever pure,
Thy judgments, true and right, endure.

More precious to the soul they are
   Than gold that from the furnace gleams;
Than honey's sweetness sweeter far,
   When newly from the comb it streams.
They duly warn Thy servant, Lord;
In keeping them is rich reward.

His errors who can understand?
   O cleanse me from my secret sin:
From daring guilt restrain my hand,
   Nor let presumption reign within,

That, harmless from the great offence,
My feet may walk in innocence.

O grant that every spoken word,
 . And every thought that stirs my mind,
May reach Thy throne of grace, O Lord,
  And in Thy sight acceptance find,
O Rock of strength, on whom I rest,
O my Redeemer, ever blest.

PSALM XX.

The Lord in thy distressful day
  Attend and hear thee still:
The mighty Name of Jacob's God
  Deliver thee from ill:

The Lord from out His holy shrine
  Discern thy needful hour,
And send thee help from Zion's height
  To stablish all thy power:

May the pure incense of thy vows
  To Him well-pleasing rise,
And in His sight accepted be
  Thy perfect sacrifice:

According to thy heart's desire
  His grace may He afford,
And all thy counsel and intent
  Be prospered of the Lord.

In thy salvation we will haste
  Our banner to display,
And praise the goodness of our God
  On thy triumphal day;

For He will His Anointed hear
  (We trust His promised grace)
And help him with His strong right hand
  From out His holy place.

In chariots some repose their hope,
  On horses some rely:
But we make mention of His Name,
  The Lord our God Most High.

They slide, they fall; but we shall rise,
  And stand with upright feet.
Save, Lord, and hear the king, whose lips
  Our choral prayer repeat.

PSALM XXI.

THE king, O Lord, with songs of praise
  Shall in Thy strength rejoice,
And, crowned with Thy salvation, raise
  To heaven his thankful voice.

For thy consent has ever blest
  The wishes of his heart,
And still, whate'er his lips request,
  Thy gracious hands impart.

Thy deeds of love are manifold,
  And all his hopes outshine;
He wears a crown of purest gold:
  The gift, O Lord, was Thine.

He prayed to Thee for life, and Thou
  Hast granted his desire;
Long life to be his portion now,
  And never to expire.

Victorious by Thy mighty aid
  His glory shines on high;
And Thou upon his head hast laid
  Honour and majesty:

He walks in joy before Thy face,
  The king of Thee beloved;
Thou art his trust, and from Thy grace
  He never shall be moved.

Thy hand shall find Thy foes, and all
  Whose hatred spurns Thy Name:
In Thy displeasure they shall fall,
  As stubble in the flame:

The Lord shall smite them in His ire;
  To fiery ruin hurled
Their race shall perish, son and sire,
  And vanish from the world.

They frame their crafty plans in vain:
  In vain against Thee fight:
Full on their front Thine arrows rain,
  And drive their hosts to flight.

O Lord, exalt on high Thy Name,
  Arise, our stalwart tower:
So shall our song declare Thy fame,
  And magnify Thy power.

PSALM XXII.

My God, my God, to Thee I cry:
  Ah, why hast Thou forsaken me?
I cry in vain: no help is nigh;
  My bitter moan I make, uncomforted by Thee.

All day I call: none answers, none:
  I groan throughout the unquiet night:
Yet Thou art still the Holy One
  Whom Israel's songs adore, throned in Thy sacred height.

Our fathers trusted in Thy Word,
  And swift Thy strong deliverance came:
They cried to Thee, their saving Lord,
  To Thee they cried in faith, and were not put to shame.

For me—a worm, no man am I;
  The very abjects on me tread:
In reckless mood the passers by
  Shoot out the flouting lip, and wag the insulting head:

'His trusted Lord,' they shout in scorn,
  'Let Him redeem His darling child.'
Yea, Thine I was, while yet unborn,
  Thine, when upon the breast in sweet repose I smiled:

Thy power, that took me from the womb,
  Shall still support me to the grave;
O shine upon me through the gloom,
  For trouble is at hand, and none is nigh to save.

Foes hem me in on every side,
  And strong as Bashan's bulls are they:
Their mouths on me they open wide,
  As gapes the hungry lion roaring for his prey.

My heart is wax, my bones unstrung;
  Like oozing water fails my breath;
My strength a withered sherd; my tongue
  Cleaves to my jaws: I sink into the dust of death.

Dogs prowl around me: foemen fierce
  With evil will against me rise;
And now my hands and feet they pierce*;
  My bones I count; on me they stare with eager eyes.

My plundered raiment they divide,
  And on my vesture cast the lot;
But in Thy succour I confide;
  Stand not aloof, O Lord; my Strength, forsake me not.

Snatch from the sword my lonely soul,
  Save when the dreaded hounds are nigh;
Wrest from the lion's fierce control;
  Yea, from the oxen's horns Thine ear has heard my cry.

So, where my brethren meet, Thy fame
  The voice of choral joy shall tell:
Praise ye the Lord, who fear His Name;
  Praise Him, O Jacob's seed, adore Him, Israel.

He hath not spurned the mourner's woe,
  Nor shut His ear, nor hid His face;
His glory to the tribes I show,
  And pay my public vows, and magnify His grace.

   * Many read 'as a lion', where the English versions have 'they pierced' or 'piercing' (my hands and my feet). One of their chief arguments is, that St Matthew and St John do not cite this verse (17) as prophetic of our Lord's passion, while they do quote v. 18.

The poor shall eat, and fill their hearts;
  Who seek the Lord, his Name shall bless:
Be cheered, ye saints: earth's farthest parts
  Shall know the Lord; His power all kindreds shall confess.

For to the Lord belongs the crown;
  The nation's mighty king is He:
Who eat earth's fatness, who bow down
  Powerless to save their lives, all bend to Him the knee.

His Name shall seed to latest seed,
  And age proclaim to listening youth:
The unborn shall His salvation read,
  And praise His glorious acts, His might, His saving truth.

PSALM XXIII.

My shepherd is the Lord: no care
  Or craving want I know:
In pastures green He feeds me, where
  The soothing waters flow:

He calls my wandering spirit back
  From paths of sin and shame,
And leads me in the righteous track,
  So holy is His Name.

I fear no evil, though my way
  Through death's dark valley lie;
Thy rod and staff are all my stay;
  Thy guiding hand is nigh:

Thy table for my feast is spread
  In sight of all my foes:
Thy cheerful oil anoints my head;
  My cup of joy o'erflows.

Still with Thy love and goodness blest
  Till life's last days are o'er,
Within Thy dwelling I shall rest,
  O Lord, for evermore.

PSALM XXIV.

THE earth and all that it contains,
  The world and every nation,
Are His, who on the ocean plains
  Hath laid its strong foundation.
Who shall ascend His holy hill?
The man whose heart reveres His will,
  Whose hands are clean before Him.

Whose lips from lying guile are free,
  God's Name profaning never,
The blessing of the Lord shall be
  Upon his head for ever;
The Lord shall guard him with His grace.
Such are the men who seek His face,
  Who seek the God of Jacob.

Lift up your heads, eternal gates,
  Arise, ye doors immortal;
For lo, the King of glory waits
  Before the heavenly portal:
Who is this King of glory? He,
The warrior strong, whom foemen flee,
  The mighty Lord in battle.

Lift up your heads, eternal gates,
  Arise, ye doors immortal;
For lo, the King of glory waits
  Before the heavenly portal.
Who is this King of glory? None
But He, the Lord of hosts alone,
  He is the King of glory.

PSALM XXV.

LORD, I lift my soul to Thee,
  And in Thee my trust repose;
Suffer not my shame to be
  Triumph to my boasting foes.
Such as seek Thee, guard from ill,
  And the causeless traitors baulk;
Teach me, Lord, to know Thy will,
  In Thy perfect way to walk.

Show me all Thy saving truth,
  Lead me to Thy blest abode,
Thou, my hope from earliest youth,
  Thou, my Saviour and my God.
Call Thy goodness, Lord, to mind;
  Muse upon Thine ancient love;
To my youthful faults be blind,
  Nor in wrath my sins reprove.

Spare my soul, in mercy spare;
  Good and righteous is the Lord:
With the erring He will bear,
  And instruct them in His word.
To the lowly He imparts
  Knowledge of His perfect way,
Guarding meek and faithful hearts
  That revere Him and obey.

All His saints the Lord shall guide
  With His truth and mercy still,
In His covenant who abide,
  And His holy laws fulfil.
Lord, my Helper and my Friend,
  For Thy Name's sake, look on me,
Pardon to my faults extend,
  To my great iniquity.

Who is he that fears the Lord?
  He will take him by the hand,
Ease unto his soul afford,
  To his seed confirm the land.
To His saints the Lord is nigh,
  Making known His secret will;
To the Lord I look, whose eye
  Guards me from ensnaring ill.

Turn to me and give me rest,
  Sad and lone I seek Thy face;
Calm the anguish of my breast,
  Help me with Thy saving grace.
All my failings, all my woes,
  View with eye compassionate;
See how many are my foes,
  And how fiercely burns their hate.

O Thou Saviour whom I love,
  Keep my soul and rescue me:
Shame me not, but let me prove
  All the bliss of trusting Thee.

Yea, O God, in Thee I trust;
  Hold me upright, guard, and bless:
Lift Thine Israel from the dust,
  Save him from his deep distress.

PSALM XXVI.

BE Thou my Judge, O Lord: I strive
In spotless innocence to live:
The Lord alone hath been my guide,
And so my footsteps cannot slide.

O try my reins and heart: Thy grace
And truth I keep before my face;
From fraud and falsehood I retreat,
Nor linger where the wicked meet.

O happy lot, with cleansèd hand
Before Thine altar, Lord, to stand,
The voice of melody to raise,
And publish all Thy wondrous praise.

Well do I love the blest abode,
The temple of the living God:
The holy place, I love it well,
Wherein Thine honour deigns to dwell.

Not with the reckless multitude,
Not with the men who thirst for blood,
Not with the sinners be my place,
Not with the bribe-polluted race;

Be mine the paths of innocence,
The grace of God my strong defence;
So shall I stand secure, and sing
With all His saints our heavenly King.

PSALM XXVII.

The Lord is my redeeming light:
  What terror shall be near?
My stronghold is the Lord of might:
  Whose onset shall I fear?

In vain they gather, one and all,
  To prey upon my life;
They stumble in their path, they fall,
  The wicked sons of strife.

Their tented army's proud display
  I mark with dauntless eye,
Nor wavers in the battle-fray
  My stedfast constancy.

One boon I ask the Lord, to be
  A hearer of His word,
A dweller in His house, to see
  The beauty of the Lord.

There may my lifelong days be spent;
  For He, in trouble's shock,
Shall hide me safe within His tent,
  And plant me on His rock.

To Him, who lifts my head on high
  Above the hostile throng,
Will I with sacrifice draw nigh,
  And praise the Lord in song.

Be merciful to me, O Lord,
  And answer when I speak;
'Seek ye my face:' O gracious word!
  Behold, Thy face I seek.

Hide not from me Thine angry face,
  Nor spurn Thy servant's vow:
O God, my Saviour once, Thy grace
  Withhold not from me now.

Father and mother may forsake;
  The Lord will yet sustain:
Teach me, O Lord, Thy way, and make
  The road of duty plain.

O save; for they that hate me lie
  In wait around my path,
With such as witness falsity;
  And furious is their wrath.

Fears hem me in; yet I shall stand:
  For faith is strong in me,
O Lord, that in the living land
  Thy goodness I shall see.

Then wait, my soul, upon the Lord,
  Thy comforter and guide;
Yea, wait, and trusting in His word,
  Strong in His strength, abide.

PSALM XXVIII.

LORD, my rock, I cry to Thee:
Turn not from me silently:
Lest, while Thou art mute, my doom
Be the darkness of the tomb.

Lend to me a gracious ear,
And my lowly crying hear,
When before Thy shrine I stand
Lifting high the suppliant hand.

Not with sinners be my place,
Not with the deceitful race,
Who, their minds intent on wrong,
Whisper peace with fawning tongue.

Pay them what their deeds have earned
From the Hand whose works they spurned;
Smite with Thy chastising rod
Souls that have not cared for God.

Blest be He, whose love is near
All my earnest vows to hear,
Blest be He, my strength, my shield:
Unto Him my heart I yield.

Yea, my heart, no more opprest,
Dances in my joyous breast,
And in grateful song runs o'er,
Praising Him for evermore.

Lord, whose powerful mercy still
Thine Anointed guards from ill,
Feed Thy flock from age to age,
Save and bless Thine heritage.

PSALM XXIX.

SING the Lord, ye sons of heaven;
Glory to the Lord be given:
Sing the Lord, His power and might,
Sing, in holy raiment bright.

Comes a Voice the waters o'er,
Mightier than their booming roar;
Comes Thy Thunder-voice abroad,
Lord of hosts, the glorious God.

Hark, the cedared heights along
On it rolls, majestic, strong,
Rending, crashing, far and wide,
All the stately forest's pride.

Terror-smitten leaps amain
Lebanon's great mountain-chain
As a calf, and Sirion's slope
Like the bounding antelope.

Heralds of that Voice on high
Fiery flashes cleave the sky:
Desert Kadesh hears and quakes,
When that Voice its silence wakes.

Hinds have felt the teeming throe,
Woods have laid their honours low;
But around His heavenly throne
'Glory, glory' sounds alone.

O'er the deluge sat the Lord,
Ever sits a King adored :
He shall send and still increase
To His people strength and peace.

PSALM XXX.

I PRAISE Thee, Lord, who o'er my foes
  Hast raised my head in triumph high,
Not slow to mark my secret woes,
  Not deaf to my desponding cry.

O Lord my God, my soul was faint,
  My feet were sinking to the grave ;
But Thou wast nigh to hear my plaint,
  To hear, to heal me, and to save.

Before the Lord in song rejoice,
  All ye his saints; his praise proclaim,
And offer still with heart and voice
  Thanksgiving to His holy Name.

A moment, and His anger dies;
  His grace is life for evermore:
At evening come the weeping eyes,
  But songs of joy when night is o'er.

In prosperous times I dared to say,
  'My mountain stands for ever sure:'
But Thou didst turn Thy face away,—
  O trouble heavy to endure!

I sought Thee, Lord, I came and sued;
  'Lord, to my suppliant voice attend:
What profit is there in my blood,
  When to the darkness I descend?

The silent dust—shall this declare
  The praises of Thy faithful Word?
Give ear, O Lord, unto my prayer;
  In mercy spare and help me, Lord.'—

My mourning Thou hast turned to glee;
  For sackcloth, gladness girds me now,
That songs of thankful praise to Thee,
  O Lord my God, may ever flow.

PSALM XXXI.

O Lord, my refuge is in Thee:
  Then never put to shame
My faithful prayer: to rescue me
  Thy plighted truth I claim.

Bow down Thy gracious ear, and now
    Deliver me with speed:
Be Thou my rock, my fortress Thou,
    To save in time of need.

Thy saving strength of old is tried;
    Thou art my rock and tower:
Then for Thy Name's sake Thou wilt guide,
    And lead me by Thy power.

Thou shalt release me from the snare
    Which crafty foes have laid:
Thou art my stronghold, all my care
    Is for Thy mighty aid.

Into Thy keeping I resign
    My soul, Thy rightful due:
Thou hast redeemed and made me Thine,
    O Lord my God most true.

O hateful race, who will not part
    From lies to be abhorred!
On vanities they set their heart:
    My trust is in the Lord.

Thy loving-kindness is my joy,
    My sorrows Thou dost see:
The evils that my soul annoy,
    They all are known to Thee.

Safe from the foeman's cruel chain,
    By Thy protecting hand
Upon a wide and open plain
    My feet in freedom stand.

Have pity, Lord: for woes assail,
  And gather round me fast;
Mine eyes for pining sorrow fail,
  My soul and body waste:

My life is worn with ceaseless moan:
  I weep mine years away:
My fainting strength is well-nigh flown,
  My very bones decay;

The taunting foes my fame belie;
  My friends are all dismayed;
Each neighbour, each familiar eye
  To see me is afraid:

Even as the dead are out of mind,
  So am I quite forgot:
As potsherds scattered to the wind,
  I am remembered not.

I heard the slanders of the crowd,
  I saw their bitter strife,
While they devised, with threatenings loud,
  To take away my life.

But still I look to Thee for aid
  And to Thy saving rod;
For I confess, and still have said,
  O Lord, Thou art my God.

My times are in Thy mighty hand,
  My life in Thy control:
O save me from the hostile band
  Who persecute my soul.

Upon Thy servant's deep distress
  O make Thy face to shine:
Preserve me in Thy righteousness,
  O Lord, for I am Thine.

O never let me suffer blame,
  But when I seek Thee, save:
And be the sinner's portion shame
  And silence in the grave.

Dumb be the lips that utter lies,
  And in disdainful mood
Pour forth their railing calumnies
  Against the just and good.

What blessings hath Thy love in store,
  Displayed to mortal sight,
For all who fear Thee and adore,
  And seek Thy saving light!

They dwell within Thy sanctuary
  Secure from human wrongs,
Beneath Thy secret tent they lie
  Far from the strife of tongues.

Blest be the goodness of the Lord,
  Whose wondrous love was shown,
Safe keeping me with watch and ward
  As in a fencèd town.

And when I said in hasty fear,
  'Far from Thy sight I lie,'
Swift was Thine ear my voice to hear
  And note my suppliant cry.

O love the Lord, ye saints: the Lord
  His faithful seed shall bless,
And measure plentiful reward
  To sinful haughtiness.

If from His faith ye ne'er depart,
  If for His peace ye long,
His joy shall gladden every heart,
  His strength shall make you strong.

PSALM XXXII.

HAPPY the man whose errors find
  The Lord's forgiving grace,
Whose deeds of wickedness are veiled
  From His reproving face:

Yea, blest is he to whom the Lord
  Will not impute his sin,
Who hides no evil in his heart
  Nor any guile within.

For while in silence and constraint
  I hid my guilty fears,
My very bones consumed away
  With pining and with tears:

All day and night my weary frame
  Thy heavy hand oppress'd;
My heart, as though with summer heat,
  Was melting in my breast:

'I will confess to Him,' I said:
  'To Him my sins display;'
And Thou forgavest, Lord; Thy grace
  Hath put my guilt away.

For this, whilst yet He may be found,
   To Him the righteous cry;
So, when the waterfloods prevail,
   Their feet shall stand on high.

When troubles hem me in, I find
   A hiding-place in Thee:
Thou puttest in my joyful mouth
   The song of liberty.

Come hither, and be taught of me
   The way to walk aright;
For I will teach and counsel well,
   And hold you in my sight.

Nor be ye like the reckless horse,
   Nor like the stubborn mule,
Whose pace without the rein and bit
   Their rider cannot rule.

The wicked man hath many plagues
   And sorrows to endure;
But unto them that trust the Lord
   His goodness standeth sure.

Be joyful therefore in the Lord;
   To Him lift up your voice:
All ye of pure and upright heart,
   Be thankful and rejoice.

PSALM XXXIII.

O REJOICE, ye righteous, in the Lord,
   It befits the meek to bless His Name:
Let the harp awake its glowing chord,
   On the ten-stringed lute exalt His fame:

With a new-made song of thankful glee
Sing ye praises to Him lustily.

All the statutes of the Lord are sooth,
  And His work is faithful evermore:
His delight is righteousness and truth,
  From His wealth the lap of earth runs o'er:
Thou hast made the heavens by Thy word,
And their armies by Thy breath, O Lord.

At His call the billows sink and swell
  In the caves of ocean treasured deep:
Fear the Lord, all ye on earth that dwell:
  Let the world before Him silence keep.
He hath spoken, and the fabric stands;
He hath willed; 'tis done as He commands.

By the Lord o'erruled and flung aside
  All the heathen plottings come to nought:
But the counsels of the Lord abide,
  And, for ever firm, His secret thought:
They are blest, His chosen seed of yore,
Who the Lord alone as God adore.

He beholdeth from His heav'nly height
  All the sons of men, their works and ways:
From His throne of everlasting light
  The wide earth is open to His gaze;
'Twas the Lord who formed the heart of man,
And His eyes alone its workings scan.

What avails a king's embattled host?
  What avails a mighty warrior's arm?
What are strong-limbed steeds? an empty boast:
  Who revere the Lord, He guards from harm;

Who attend His love with child-like faith
He will feed in dearth, and save from death.

For the Lord's salvation we will wait;
　For our shield is He, our strong defence;
And the gladness of their hearts is great,
　Who repose beneath His Providence.
For the faithful Lord will surely bless
Every soul that trusts His faithfulness.

PSALM XXXIV.

Ever will I bless the Lord,
　And His endless glory speak,
I will praise Him, and my word
　Shall be gladness to the meek.

Let the Lord be magnified;
　Let us all extol His Name:
When I called Him, He replied,
　And His swift deliverance came.

When the meek His aid implore,
　Light will dawn upon their eyes:
All the mourner's woes are o'er,
　When the Lord hath heard his cries.

Round His saints, to guard and guide,
　Camps the angel of the Lord,
And their wants are all supplied
　Who revere and keep His Word.

Taste and see; the Lord is good:
　Fear Him, ye His holy seed:
When the lions pine for food,
　They that seek Him nothing need.

Come, ye children, list to me,
    And be taught the Lord's true fear.
Life and honour who would see,
    And long days of sweetness here?

Keep thy lips from cunning sleight,
    And thy tongue from speaking ill:
Hate the wrong, and do the right;
    Follow peace with stedfast will.

For the Lord beholds the just,
    And in mercy hears their cry;
Sinners, trampled in the dust,
    Fade beneath His angry eye.

To His saints the Lord is kind,
    For their trouble swift to feel,
Swift the broken heart to bind,
    And the contrite spirit heal.

Many woes the meek has known,
    But the Lord redeems from all,
And without a shattered bone
    Bids him rise from every fall.

Death awaits the wicked seed,
    Judgment them that hate the just:
But from death and judgment freed
    In the Lord His servants trust.

PSALM XXXV. Part I.

Strive with my striving foes, O Lord,
    And them that smite me smite:
Take hold of shield and buckler, rise
    To guard my perilled right.

Against my fierce pursuer's rage
    Draw forth the spear, and stand:
Say to my soul, 'Behold, I come:
    Salvation is at hand.'

Be they dismayed and put to shame,
    Who hunt my guiltless life;
Defeated be their cunning plots,
    And quelled their cruel strife:

Swift let them fly, the routed foes,
    As chaff before the wind;
Swift be the angel of the Lord
    To scatter them behind:

All dark and slippery be their path,
    And with avenging sword
Fast follow on their wildered flight
    The angel of the Lord.

They dug a pit to trap my soul;
    They laid a causeless snare:
In their own mischief let them fall,
    And perish unaware.

So shall my soul in Him rejoice,
    In His salvation rest;
And all my bones shall say, 'The Lord,
    The mighty Lord, be blest'.

For who is like, O Lord, to Thee,
    By whom the weak are freed
From tyrant's power, and needy men
    Escape the spoiler's greed?

False witnesses arose, and spake
  Of things to me unknown:
They paid me evil for my good,
  And left me sad and lone.

Yet, clad in sackcloth, worn with fasts,
  When they were sick, I mourned;
And many an interceding prayer
  Into my lap returned.

As they were friends, or brethren dear,
  Myself I did behave:
As one who weeps in mournful plight
  Upon a mother's grave.

And now rejoicing in my woe
  They come; the abject tribe,
Men whom I knew not, gathered round
  And aimed the cruel gibe:

The vile buffoons, whose scurril tongues
  Procure them daily bread,
Laughed loud on me with gnashing teeth,
  And wagged the scornful head.

PART II.

How long art silent, Lord? how long
Regards Thy patient eye my wrong?
Save from the lion's fierce control,
O save my lone afflicted soul.

So, where the tribes adore Thy Name,
My song Thy glory shall proclaim,
And listening crowds shall learn to bless
Thy wondrous love and faithfulness.

Let them not gladden with my woes
Their causeless hate, the haughty foes,
Against the peaceful who prepare
The bitter scoff, the treacherous snare.

Their mouths on me they open wide:
'Aha', they say, 'our eyes espied':
Lord, Thou hast seen: Thy silence break,
Stand not aloof; arise, awake.

Judge Thou my cause, my God and Lord;
Maintain me by Thy stedfast word,
Give sentence for my righteous suit,
And bid the exulting foe be mute.

Let not their persecuting spite,
O Lord my God, defeat my right:
Let them not shout: 'Our wish is won;
Lo where he lies, o'erthrown, undone'.

Be all, who make my woes their scorn,
Abased, afflicted, and forlorn:
Who trample on my guiltless fame,
Contempt be theirs and withering shame.

But they who look with favouring eye
Upon my righteous cause, shall cry
With choral joy from every side,
And shout, 'The Lord be magnified'.

The Lord, of whom alone is health,
Has pleasure in His servant's wealth:
Him all the day my songs shall bless,
My tongue shall speak His righteousness.

PSALM XXXVI.

REBELLION rankles in the scorner's mind:
  The fear of God is not before his eyes:
  He feeds his foolish heart with flattering lies,
To sin's foul guilt and hateful issues blind.

Deceit and wickedness are on his tongue;
  Wisdom and goodness he has put away:
  He ponders evil plots by night and day;
In paths perverse he walks, nor hates the wrong.

The heavens, O Lord, Thy loving-kindness know;
  Thy faithfulness extends unto the sky:
  Thy truth is like the hills of God on high,
Thy judgments like the mighty deeps below.

To man and beast deliverance comes from Thee:
  How precious are Thy tender mercies, Lord!
  A refuge safe Thy shading wings afford,
To which the sons of men in peril flee.

The fatness of Thy house o'erjoys their heart,
  The river of Thy pleasures brims their cup:
  Before Thy face the stream of life wells up:
Thy light alone can light to us impart.

To such as love Thee, still vouchsafe Thy grace,
  And to the true of heart Thy faithfulness:
  Ne'er let the foot of pride upon me press,
Nor wicked hand remove me from my place.

But let the evil-doers prostrate fall,
  Cast down and trampled, never more to rise:
  And blest be He, whose glory fills the skies,
God—Father, Son and Spirit—All in All.

PSALM XXXVII. PART I.

Fret not for the evil-doers;
 View them not with envious eye:
Like the grass, they wait the mower:
 Like the leaves, they fade and die.

Trust the Lord, and do thy duty:
 Fearless in the land abide,
Glad in Him, whose faithful mercies
 All thou askest will provide.

To the Lord commit thy burden:
 Trust Him; He will act for thee;
He will clear thy truth, as daylight,
 And, as noon, thine equity.

Rest upon the Lord in patience;
 Fret not for the lucky man,
Who, secure in worldly wisdom,
 Brings to bear each crafty plan.

Not in wrath and guilty malice
 With the pampered sinner strive:
He shall perish, but the faithful,
 Waiting for the Lord, shall live.

Pause awhile:—where now the wicked?
 Seek him, he is found no more:
But the meek the land inherit,
 Peace is theirs in plenteous store.

Gnashing with his teeth the sinner
 Plots the godly soul to slay:
But the Lord derides his fury,
 For He sees his coming day.

Though the wicked bare the falchion,
  Though they bend the deadly bow,
To cast down the patient mourner,
  And the needy to lay low;

Vain their rage against the righteous,
  All their crafty schemes are vain;
Their own heart the sword shall enter,
  And their bow shall snap in twain.

Better is a good man's little
  Than the wicked's large increase;
For the Lord disarms the sinner,
  While the upright walk in peace.

He will note the daily perils,
  Guard the fortunes of the good;
Evil times shall never shame them,
  Dearth shall never stint their food;

But the godless race shall vanish,
  All whose sins the Lord provoke,
As the lamb-delighting herbage,
  As in air the gliding smoke.

Sinners borrow but repay not,
  Saints will give with generous hand:
Whom He curseth fade and perish,
  Whom He blesseth hold the land.

Part II.

LORD, Thou wilt guard with faithful love
The just man, whom Thine eyes approve;
Thy hand his footsteps will sustain,
And, if he fall, uplift again.

I have been young, and now am old,
Yet ne'er did I the meek behold
Of heaven abandoned, or his seed
Imploring at my gate for bread:

The good man's heart with pity glows:
The bounty that his hand bestows
Descends upon his distant race
In fruitful showers of heavenly grace.

Depart from ill, to good incline
Thy soul, and endless life be thine:
The Lord, to whom the truth is dear,
Forsakes no pious worshipper.

Soon shall His everlasting doom
The sinner and his race consume,
While happier saints from age to age
Possess His promised heritage.

Blest is the mouth by wisdom taught,
The good man's tongue, with justice fraught:
The law of God, his inward guide,
Forbids his stedfast feet to slide.

In vain, the righteous soul to slay,
Their treacherous snares the godless lay:
The Lord will snatch him from the grave,
And in the judgment rise to save.

Wait on the Lord; observe His ways;
The Lord thy head aloft shall raise,
Give thee the land, and in thy sight
The lawless foe with vengeance smite.

I saw the sinner: bold was he,
Strong as a green far-spreading tree:
I came again, his pride was o'er;
I sought him; he was found no more.

Behold the just and perfect: theirs
Is peace at last, and hope of heirs:
But sinners in the end decay;
The wicked have no future day.

The Lord defends the righteous seed;
He keeps them safe in time of need:
Safe from the cruel and unjust
He keeps them, for in Him they trust.

PSALM XXXVIII.

Not in Thy fury, Lord, reprove,
  Nor in Thy wrath chastise:
Too keen Thine arrows sink; Thy hand
  Too heavy on me lies.

So sore Thy blows, no soundness dwells
  My fainting frame within:
There is no quiet in my bones
  By reason of my sin:

My guilt o'erflows my head, a weight
  Too grievous to be borne;
By noisome wounds, of folly bred,
  O'ermastered and outworn,

All day I writhe and mourn, my loins
  With burning pain opprest;
Feeble and bruised I cry aloud
  In sorrowful unrest.

O Lord, my need is known to Thee:
  Thou notest all my sighs,
My throbbing heart, my failing strength,
  My wan and rayless eyes.

My friends and lovers shun my plague;
  My kinsmen stand afar,
While foemen plot against my life,
  And spread the cruel snare.

They talk of mischief, how to make
  My lonely soul a prey;
They sit and meditate deceit
  Throughout the livelong day:

They rave, as to a deaf man's ear,
  Unnoted and unheard:
I rest in silence, as the dumb,
  Nor speak one bitter word.

O Lord, in Thee my hope is strong,
  For still, what time I cried,
Thine answer came, O Lord my God.
  'Lest they be magnified,

Lest they rejoice,' I said, 'who wait
  My slipping foot to see.'
Alas, with halting steps I walk,
  And falter wearily,

While, mourning for remembered sin,
  My backward eyes I cast,
And self-condemned, my contrite lips
  Deplore the guilty past.

Ah! great in number are my foes,
   In strength and spirit great:
They render evil for my good,
   And for my kindness hate.

Forsake me not, O Lord my God,
   Stand not aloof from me;
But haste to help me, Lord, and still
   My strong salvation be.

PSALM XXXIX.

METHOUGHT I must be still
   Before the scoffer, and refrain
My tongue from good or ill;
   And long I bore my silent pain:
At length the kindling fire outbrake
From my sad bosom, and I spake:

'Lord, let me know mine end,
   Teach me the measure of my days:
The life on earth I spend,
   How soon its little light decays.
A cypher are my times with Thee:
For man at best is vanity.

Man is a shade; no more:
   He is disquieted in vain:
He heaps his wealthy store,
   And knows not whose shall be the gain.
What trust I then?—Thy gracious Word.—
Release me from my sins, O Lord.

Lest fools deride, I stand
    Silent and calm beneath Thy blow:
Yet hold Thy smiting hand:
    For, when Thou chastenest sin with woe,
Our joyless life is worn away,
And men, as by the moth, decay.

Lord, hearken to my prayer,
    Give ear unto my weeping cry;
Even as my fathers were,
    A pilgrim in the world am I.
Then frown no more, but cheer and bless
My parting from this wilderness."

PSALM XL.

I waited for a gentle word
    Of comfort from the Lord:
He hung a gracious ear He bent
    Unto my sad lament,
And from the pit of sore dire.
    And from the whelming mire
My feet He lifted on a rock,
    Secure from every shock.

A joyful song He bade me sing,
    A song of holy praise:
Many shall see it, and adore
    The Lord with pious fear.
Happy, who makes the Lord his trust,
    Nor wanders with the unjust
In slippery paths, where vain doubt
    Beguiles his sliding foot.

O Lord my God, how bright they shine,
  Thy works of power divine!
Thine acts how wondrous we behold,
  Thy love how manifold!
With Thine what deeds shall we compare?
  What mortal tongue may dare
The unimagined to express,
  Or count the numberless?

To Thee no sacrifice is dear
  (Thus openest Thou mine ear);
Incense and offerings for sin
  With Thee no favour win:
Then said I, 'Lo I come, my God,
  Thy Volume's written code
Obeying with my heart, and still
  Intent to do Thy will.'

Among the tribes I will proclaim
  Thy mercy-loving Name:
Yea, Lord, Thou know'st, I will not close
  My lips in mute repose,
Nor in my sluggish heart suppress
  Thy saving righteousness,
But tell Thy love, Thy truth, abroad,
  O good and faithful God.

Hide not, O Lord, Thy shining face,
  But guard me with Thy grace:
Dark waves of anguish o'er me roll;
  The sins that wring my soul
Exceed the hairs upon my head;
  My life is sore bestead,
Mine eyes are dimmed, my spirits flee,
  And my heart faileth me.

Haste Thee to help, O Lord; o'erthrow
  The workers of my woe;
Who seek my life with treacherous aim
  Be theirs defeat and shame,
Contempt be theirs, and headlong flight,
  And troubles infinite,
Who shout 'Aha' with taunting voice,
  And in my pain rejoice.

But happy they who seek Thy face,
  Who bless Thy saving grace,
And cry: 'The Lord is on our side;
  The Lord be magnified.'
In days of poverty and grief
  I wait the Lord's relief:
Saviour and Guardian of my lot,
  My God, O tarry not.

PSALM XLI.

Blest he, whose timely mercies heed
  The poor man's need!
His guardian Lord shall save him still
  From every ill:
Among the living he shall rest,
And with the land's increase be blest.

Thou wilt not leave him comfortless
  When foes oppress;
Low though he lie with pining breath,
  And nigh to death,
Thy hand will prop his sinking head,
And in his sickness smoothe his bed.

O Lord, I cried, new mercy show,
  New health bestow;
For heavy lies the weight of sin
  My heart within:
'When will he die,' my foemen say,
'And his remembrance fade away?'

If any see me, they devise
  Ensnaring lies:
The venom in their bosoms bred
  Abroad they shed;
My haters whisper, and contrive
How they may swallow me alive.

'His many crimes,' they say, 'provoke
  The deadly stroke;
Lo, on his bed of pain he lies,
  No more to rise.'
The very friend, who shared my cup,
His heel against me lifteth up.

But I Thy mercy will implore:
  O Lord, restore
And raise me, that I may requite
  Their cruel spite.
Herein wilt Thou Thy favour show,
That foes exult not in my woe.

Thou wilt maintain with strong defence
  Mine innocence,
And keep me still before Thy face
  With endless grace.
Praise we the Lord for evermore,
The God whom Israel's sons adore.

PSALM XLII.

As pants the hart for cooling streams,
   So longs my soul for Thee,
O God; my heart is all athirst
   The living God to see.

When shall I stand before His face?
   Tears are my meat by day,
And tears by night: 'Where now thy God?'
   The busy mockers say.

Of bygone days I dream, and pour
   My soul in lonely woe;—
How oft I led the holy throng
   With solemn step and slow;

How to the house of God we went,
   And in His glorious hall
With hymns of praise and choral joy
   We kept high festival.

Why art thou downcast, O my soul?
   Why trembling with affright?
Hope thou in God: the time shall come
   To bless His healing light.

O God, my soul is bowed with care,
   And pineth for Thee still
From Jordan's springs, from Hermon's crests,
   And Mitsar's humbler hill.

Deep calleth unto deep: aloud
   Thy spouting tempest raves;
And o'er me swells Thy billowy surge,
   The might of all Thy waves.

God's daily grace shall yet be mine,
  His song my nightly joy,
Yea, prayer to God, who guards my life,
  My only sweet employ.

O God my rock, I cry to Thee;
  Am I forgotten quite?
Still must I mourn, still quail beneath
  The proud oppressor's spite?

My haters say, 'Where now thy God?'
  O keen and cruel word!
Through all my bones with murderous dint
  It stabbeth like a sword.

Why art thou downcast, O my soul?
  Why trembling in my breast?
O place thy hope in God: on Him
  Recline, and be at rest:

For surely I shall thank Him yet
  Within His blest abode,
Who shines on me with healing light,
  My own, my faithful God.

PSALM XLIII.

JUDGE me, O God; maintain my cause
  Against the spiteful throng;
Defend me from the lawless hand
  And from the lying tongue.

O Thou that art my saving God,
  Why am I cast away?
Why bear I thus the proud man's wrong,
  And mourn the livelong day?

Send forth Thy guiding light and truth,
  And bring me by Thy grace
Unto the mountain of Thy strength,
  Thy holy dwelling-place:

Where to Thy altar I may come,
  O God, my joy, my cheer,
And praise Thee on the swelling harp,
  O God, my God most dear.

Why art thou downcast, O my soul?
  Why trembling in my breast?
O place thy hope in God: on Him
  Recline, and be at rest:

For surely I shall thank Him yet
  Within His blest abode,
Who shines on me with healing light,
  My own, my faithful God.

PSALM XLIV.

OFT have we heard our fathers tell,
  O God, Thy wondrous works and ways,
  Thy marvels wrought in olden days,
How by Thy hand the heathen fell,

Of fruitful Canaan dispossest,
  And Israel entered in their room:
  They dying by a fearful doom,
Whilst ours in towering strength increast.

Yet won they not that pleasant land
  By their own swords; their own brave arm
  Protected not their life from harm,
But Thy right arm, Thy mighty hand.

Yea, by the brightness of Thy face
  And by Thy favour they o'ercame.
  My King and God, O still the same,
Salvation send to Jacob's race.

For by Thine aid our enemies
  Lay prostrate on the purple ground;
  And in Thy Name we still confound
The bands who dare against us rise.

Our swords are powerless to defend;
  We trust not in our fragile bows:
  Thou, Lord, hast saved us from our foes,
And brought them to a shameful end.

For this with praises we delight
  To bless God's ever glorious Name;
  But now Thou yieldest us to shame,
Nor leadest forth our hosts to fight.

Our faces from the foe reversed,
  A spoil to such as hunt for blood,
  Thou givest us like sheep for food,
Among the heathen tribes dispersed.

For nought dost Thou Thy people sell,
  Nor art enrichèd by the price:
  Our neighbours in our fall rejoice,
A scorn to all who near us dwell,

A byword to the heathen grown,
  Who shake their heads at our disgrace:
  My shame is still before my face,
Mine eyes to earth with blushes thrown:

So fierce the bold blasphemer's taunt,
   The proud avenger's threatening look;
   Yet Thee, O Lord, we ne'er forsook,
Nor falsified Thy covenant.

Our hearts have not forsworn their faith,
   Our steps decline not from Thy way,
   Though crushed by Thee, where jackals prey
And covered with the shade of death.

For should we from the Lord depart,
   And lift to idol gods the hand,
   Would not our sin by Him be scanned,
Who reads the secrets of the heart?

For thy sake daily we are slain,
   For slaughter marked like fatted sheep;
   Awake, O Lord; yet dost Thou sleep?
Arise, nor us for aye disdain.

O to Thine own at length return:
   Why wilt Thou hide Thy gladdening face,
   Withdrawing Thine accustomed grace
From hearts that in affliction mourn?

Our souls are prostrate in the dust,
   And to the ground our bellies cleave;
   O for Thy mercy's sake relieve,
Redeem us, Lord, our strength and trust.

PSALM XLV.

My heart is full, and I must sing:
   My heart with praise is swelling;
And I must sing unto the King
   A song His honour telling.

O fairer Thou than mortal race,
Thy lips o'erflow with heavenly grace,
  And so Thou art confessèd
  Of God for ever blessèd.

Gird on Thy sword, most Mighty; take
  Thy majesty and glory;
Ride on for truth and meekness' sake,
  Ride on, while saints adore Thee.
Dread marvels shall Thy right hand show,
Sharp fall Thine arrows on the foe,
  O God, who ever reignest,
  And equity maintainest.

Thou hatest wickedness, of right
  A lover pure and zealous:
With oil of joy Thy locks are bright;
  For God above Thy fellows,
Thy God, anoints Thee: cassia's scent,
Myrrh, aloes, with Thy robes are blent:
  With music's mingled voices
  Thine ivory dome rejoices.

Kings' daughters in Thy court are seen,
  The pride of many a nation,
And, bright with Ophir's gold, the Queen
  At Thy right hand in station.
O daughter, lend a willing ear,
And rest in sweet contentment here,
  Thy land no more regretting,
  Thy father's house forgetting.

The King elects thee for His Bride:
  Incline thy heart to hear Him:
Thy former fancies cast aside:
  He is thy Lord: revere Him.

So shall thy beauty be His choice,
So in thy love shall He rejoice;
   Tyre's daughter shall implore thee,
   And kneel with gifts before thee.

She comes in gold and broidered sheen;
   Her virgin mates attend her;
To the King's palace comes the Queen
   In pomp of festal splendour.
Instead of sires through all the land
Thy sons shall rule, a princely band,
   And minstrels shall deliver
   Thy praise to live for ever.

PSALM XLVI.

GOD is our sure defence, our aid
   In time of tribulation:
Our heart shall never be dismayed,
   Though fail the earth's foundation;
O'er hills though foaming floods ascend,
Though billows roar, and ocean rend
   The mountain-peaks asunder.

A river by the holy shrine,
   A pure and lovely river,
Makes glad the seat of power divine:
   She stands unmoved for ever;
For God is in the midst of her;
A help, a stay, a comforter,
   He comes at break of morning.

In Jacob's God our strength is found,
   When heathen hosts assemble:
He speaks in thunder; at the sound
   Earth melts and nations tremble:

The Lord of hosts a refuge stands,
And lo, the wonders of his hands,
  The wrath, the desolation!

He lulls the war, He burns the car,
  The bow and spear He breaketh:
Be still, He cries, for I arise:
  The Lord, the Lord awaketh
O'er all the earth a God most High:
The Lord of hosts, our help, is nigh,
  Our strength, the God of Jacob.

PSALM XLVII.

ALL ye people, come, and clap your hands;
  Unto God with shouts of triumph sing:
For the Lord is feared in utmost lands,
  The Most High is known, a mighty King.

He hath trodden out the heathen's rage,
  He hath laid the nations at our feet:
And His Jacob's beauteous heritage
  Is the land He loves, His chosen seat.

God is gone up with a merry noise,
  The Lord with the trumpet's swelling mirth:
To our King give praise; in God rejoice,
  For our God is King of all the earth.

On His holy hill He sits enthroned,
  And the heathen bow beneath His rod:
Let His Name with heart and voice be owned,
  With a song of wisdom praise our God.

Unto Abraham's God their princes call,
  With His people's host their hosts ally:
For the shields of earth God marshals all,
  Over all He reigns, a King most High.

PSALM XLVIII.

GREAT the Lord, with glorious light
Shining from His holy height
In the city of our God!
Zion there, the King's abode,

Towers upon the northern side,
Beauteous mount, our joy and pride:
God within her courts is known,
God the refuge of His own.

Kings of earth, to war arrayed,
Came and saw and shrank afraid;
Trembling seized them, pangs and woes,
Like a woman in her throes.

When Thine east-winds rend the sky,
Ships of Tarshish broken lie.
As from olden fame we heard
Such before our eyes appeared,

Lord of hosts, Thy bright abode
In the city of our God,
Stablished by His hand to be
God's own house eternally.

For Thy goodness, God of grace,
Praying in Thy holy place,
Wait we ever: as Thy Name
Far, O God, extends Thy fame:

Utmost lands Thy right hand bless
Rich with gifts of righteousness:
Sweet Thy law to Zion's hill,
Gladdening Judah's daughters still.

Walk round Zion's holy bowers,
Number all her stately towers:
Noting each embattled wall,
Gazing on each brilliant hall,

To the coming age make known:
'This God is our God alone,
Guarding us to life's last breath,
Guiding through the shades of death.'

PSALM XLIX.

HEAR, O ye nations of the earth,
   All people of the world, give ear:
Ye men of low and noble birth,
   Ye rich and poor, together hear.

Sage doctrine from my lips shall flow,
   My thoughtful heart, no longer mute,
Old truth in parables will show,
   And sing deep wisdom on the lute.

Why should I fear the evil hour,
   When cruel foes in ambush lie,
Who revel in their pride of power,
   And on their hoarded wealth rely?

A brother's ransom who can pay,
   Or alter God's eternal doom?
What hand shall wrest from death his prey,
   Its banquet from the rotting tomb?

So frail a hope, such fruitless cost,
  The rich must lay for ever by;
And weak, he sees, is wisdom's boast;
  The learned with the simple die.

But oft in secret heart they deem
  Their houses undisturbed shall stand;
Of lasting homes they fondly dream,
  And give their titles to the land.

How vain the thoughts of human pride!
  How little do they muse on death!
Man in his wealth shall not abide,
  But, like the beast, he perisheth.

Yet still their idle faith they keep,
  And children walk the self-same way;
They hasten to the tomb like sheep,
  And death consumes his early prey.

At morn the righteous tread the place,
  Where fade their splendours in the grave;
But me my God's redeeming grace
  From that dark prison-house shall save.

Dread not the rich man's growing sway:
  Will grandeur shun the stroke of doom?
He dies, and takes no wealth away,
  No glory lights that endless gloom.

Then let the rich his store enjoy,
  Use, while they last, his prosperous days,
In pleasure's chase his thoughts employ,
  And love the flatterer's selfish praise:

All soon is over; soon he lies
   With sires asleep in lightless death.
A man in honour, but unwise,
   Is like the beast that perisheth.

PSALM L.

HE hath spoken : God, the mighty Lord, hath
      spoken :
   From the sun's rising to his setting light
   He cries to earth: from Zion's peerless height
The glorious splendour of her God hath broken.

He comes, no longer mute : before Him flitteth
   Devouring fire; strong tempests round Him fly:
   He calls the earth, He calls the heaven on high:
Now on His throne, the people's Judge, He sitteth.

'Hither,' He saith, 'My chosen saints assemble,
   Who made their peace with Me by sacrifice.'
   God speaks in judgment: let the starry skies
Declare His righteousness; earth hear and tremble.

'Israel, My people, hearken: I who cite thee,
   Am God, thy worshipped God; before My shrine
   Thy costly flames of incense ever shine ;
Not for the stint of victims will I smite thee.

But steer and slaughtered he-goat cannot sway Me:
   No gift of thine from stall or fold I take:
   For every beast is Mine that haunts the brake,
The cattle on a thousand hills obey Me.

I count the birds that skim the breezy mountains;
   The roamers of the field are known to Me:
   If I am hungry, need I call on thee?
The world is Mine with all its fruits and fountains.

I crave nor bull nor goat: with praise address Me:
  Such vows unto the Highest fitly pay;
  So, if thou cry to Me in trouble's day,
Saved by My love, thy grateful songs shall bless Me.'

God saith unto the wicked: 'Thou pretendest
  To prize My covenant, and to preach My Word,
  Yet still by thee correction is abhorred;
Against My statutes daily thou offendest.

Thou smilest on a thief, thy share receiving:
  Beside the foul adulterer is thy place:
  Thy lips are fluent to defend the base,
Thy tongue expert in lying and deceiving.

I heard thee stab thy brother's reputation,
  Thy mother's son with venomed slander strike;
  And I was mute: then saidst thou God was like
Thy wicked self: O vile imagination!

But I will smite thee soon, thou evil-liver,
  And order all thy sin before thine eyes.
  O now, ye God-forgetting seed, be wise,
Lest I should cast you down, and none deliver.

A true thanksgiving is My choice oblation:
  The prayer of grateful hearts is heard above:
  Who lives to Me by holy faith and love,
He in the end shall see his God's salvation.'

PSALM LI.

O GOD, have mercy upon me,
  According to Thy wonted grace;
And let Thy kindness, full and free,
  The blot of all my guilt efface.

O wash me from my wickedness,
   And cleanse me from my sinful stain:
My great transgression I confess;
   My heart is wrung with ceaseless pain.

I sinned against Thy Holy Word,
   And did such evil in Thy sight
As stamps the sinner's act abhorred,
   And shows Thy judgment true and right.

For what am I? conceived in sin,
   And born of erring flesh and blood:
But lo, Thou lovest truth within,
   Thy warning tells me what is good.

With hyssop Thou shalt make me pure,
   To snowy whiteness wash my soul,
With gladdening words my sorrow cure,
   And bid the broken bones be whole.

Hide from my sins, O God, Thy face;
   Blot out my foul iniquity;
Give me a heart made clean by grace,
   A soul renewed, and strong in Thee.

Cast me not from Thee, nor remove
   Thy Holy Spirit's guiding voice;
Still let me feel Thy present love,
   Still in Thy saving power rejoice.

So to a lost and lawless seed
   Thy message shall my lips proclaim,
Till wakened sinners learn to heed
   Thy ways, and bless Thy holy Name.

Cleanse me from blood, my tongue shall praise
    Thy goodness, O my saving God:
Ope Thou my lips, my mouth shall blaze
    Thy glory to the world abroad.

Burnt sacrifice delights Thee not,
    Or all my flocks and herds were Thine;
The flesh of ram, the blood of goat,
    They find no welcome at Thy shrine.

A broken spirit's inward smart,
    Such is Thy chosen sacrifice:
A broken and a contrite heart,
    O God, Thou never wilt despise.

Bless Zion, Lord; build Salem's wall,
    That perfect lambs may feed Thy flame,
Yea, bullocks at Thine altar fall,
    And holy crowds adore Thy Name.

PSALM LII.

WHY vauntest thou thy mischief, man of might,
    When day by day the grace of God abides?
    Thy tongue, that plotteth harm, as smoothly glides
As the keen razor's edge, thou hypocrite.

Evil is sweeter far than good to thee,
    And lying more than truth thy daily joy:
    Thy words are uttered only to destroy,
O tongue of malice and dark treachery.

But soon shall God uproot thee; from thy seat
    He plucks thee forth for ever; thou shalt be
    Rent from the living: this the just shall see
With holy fear, and laugh at thy defeat.

Lo, this the man who made not God his fort,
  But trusted in his wealth, and stoutly trod
  The paths of wickedness! For me—O God,
Like the green olive planted in Thy court,

I trust Thy saving grace for evermore:
  Still will I bless Thee for Thy tender love,
  Still hope in Thy great Name, which saints
    above
With saints on earth in concord sweet adore.

PSALM LIII.*

Fools in their dreaming fancies still
  Declare there is no God, the while
They pamper their rebellious will,
  Nor deem whate'er delights them vile,
  Their souls with evil thoughts defile,
And all their worst desires fulfil.

God from the highest heaven His eyes
  On human thoughts and actions threw,
Nor one beheld beneath the skies,
  Who sought Him, or His statutes knew;
  Vice all with strong intent pursue,
But none forsaken virtue prize.

O deaf to good, in knowledge blind,
  By sin through mists of error led,
O sensual bodies, void of mind,
  Too dull the wrath of heaven to dread!
  God's people they devour like bread:
God's light on them hath never shined.

* This Psalm (nearly identical with Ps. 14) is chiefly given as paraphrased by George Sandys.

Their heart vain terrors shall affright,
  Their sleep be scared by guilty fear;
Their bones shall God asunder smite,
  Who impious arms against Him rear:
  Foul infamy their names shall sear,
Abhorrèd in His holy sight.

Thy chosen people to sustain
  Let gracious light from Zion spring:
The foeman's rage if God refrain,
  And Jacob out of bondage bring,
  Then, Lord, Thy greatness we shall sing,
And Israel's joy will bloom again.

PSALM LIV.

SAVE me through Thy Name, O God,
Right me with Thy potent rod:
Hear my prayer, in mercy hear;
To my words, O God, give ear.

For my foes in anger hot
Hunt my life with many a plot;
All the proud against me rise:
God is not before their eyes.

But the Lord upholds my life:
God defeats their impious strife:
Faithful ever to His plight
Them that smite me God shall smite.

With a freewill offering,
Thanks, O Lord, to Thee I sing:
For Thou quellest all my woes,
For Thou treadest down my foes.

PSALM LV.

Give ear to me, O God;
  Hide not Thy face away;
Look on me from Thy bright abode,
  And answer when I pray.

I wander to and fro;
  With restless sighs I mourn,
In terror of the raging foe,
  The proud maligner's scorn.

Their fierce and angry will
  Is bent to work my bale:
My heart with deadly fear is chill,
  My trembling spirits fail.

When doubt my bosom wrings,
  And horrid thoughts affright,
'Were mine,' I cry, 'the dove's light wings,
  How would I speed my flight!

How hasten far away,
  And in the desert dwell,
Safe from the stormy whirlwind's sway,
  The tempest's angry swell!'

Their stern decrees annul;
  Their counsels, Lord, divide;
For lo, the city streets are full
  Of violence and pride.

Mischief and guilty wrong
  Within her gates abound:
By day and night her walls along
  They pace their hateful round.

Unrighteousness and sin
  Sit there in princely seat;
Falsehood and fraud abide therein,
  And prowl in every street.

Were this a foeman's spite,
  I could endure the woe:
Were hands that hate me raised to smite,
  I might have shunned the blow:

But thou, my comrade tried,
  My friend, with whom I trod,
In sweet communion, side by side,
  The peopled house of God!—

Be theirs swift death to die,
  A living grave to fill,
Whose treacherous hearts conceive a lie,
  Whose dwellings teem with ill.

When to my God I pray,
  The Lord's strong help is nigh:
At morn, at noon, at closing day
  He notes my doleful cry.

He saves me from my foes
  In the keen battle-strife,
Though they be many that oppose,
  And hunt my guiltless life.

He from His ancient throne
  Hears, and with chastening rod
Afflicts the sinners, who live on
  In guilt, and fear not God.

Against the righteous band,
  Whose souls in peace delight,
The scorner lifts his armèd hand,
  And breaks his solemn plight.

War in his heart the while,
  He speaks with gentlest words,
As butter smooth, more soft than oil;
  Yet are they naked swords.

Cast on the Lord thy care;
  With His sustaining grace
God will uphold the just, nor e'er
  Remove him from his place.

The men of guile and blood
  Not half their days shall see,
The reeking pit their doom:—O God,
  My trust I place in Thee.

PSALM LVI.

O GOD, be merciful to me;
  The panting foeman hunts my life:
All day my timid footsteps flee
  Before his unrelenting strife:
All day fierce crowds beset my path,
With pride elate, and hot with wrath.

But when grim terrors shake me most,
  Thy promise is my sure defence:
Of God alone I make my boast,
  In God I place my confidence.
If God be nigh, what foe can harm?
What fear I from the fleshly arm?

They wrest my words the livelong day;
  Their thoughts are all to work me woe:
They dog my steps, intent to slay,
  In secret ambush crouching low.
And shall the guilty scape Thy rod?
Rise in Thy wrath, and smite, O God.

Take note of all my dismal fears;
  Upon my restless flittings look;
Within Thy bottle store my tears:—
  Are they not written in Thy book?
Full well I know, my foes shall flee,
What time I call, my God, on Thee.

For, when grim terrors shake me most,
  Thy promise is my sure defence:
Of God the Lord I make my boast,
  In God I place my confidence.
If God be nigh, what foe can harm?
What fear I from the fleshly arm?

Thy vows, O God, upon me lie:
  My glad thank-offerings I will pay:
For thou hast set my feet on high,
  Nor left my soul to death a prey:
That I may walk before Thy sight,
A tenant of the living light.

PSALM LVII.

BE merciful to me, O God,
  Be merciful to me,
My soul's retreat, my safe abode,
  Thy shading wings shall be:

Until the wicked cease from wrong,
  I call on the Most High;
I call on God, my Saviour strong,
  Whose help is ever nigh.

God will send forth from heaven above,
  And shame my ravening foes;
God will send forth His truth and love,
  And bid my soul repose.

I dwell with lions: fiery hearts
  Around my pillow throng:
Their teeth are spears and wingèd darts,
  A whetted sword their tongue.

Arise, and show Thyself, O God,
  Above the heavenly height;
Exalt Thy Name on earth abroad,
  Thy majesty and might.

They dug a pit, a net prepared
  To trap my careless feet:
But in their own devices snared
  They rue the vain deceit.

My heart is fixed, O God, my heart
  Is fixed to sing Thy praise:
My tongue shall bear its joyful part,
  And give Thee thanks always.

Awake, my glory; with the day,
  My lute and harp, awake:
For I will up and tune my lay
  Ere early morning break.

Among the people I will bless,
　O Lord, Thy saving Name,
To heathen lands Thy righteousness
　In grateful song proclaim.

Thy loving mercy soars as far
　As highest heaven is high,
Beyond the light of any star
　That shineth in the sky.

Arise, and show Thyself, O God,
　Above the heavenly height:
Exalt Thy Name on earth abroad,
　Thy majesty and might.

PSALM LVIII.

YE silent rulers, are your judgments just?
And is your sentence right, ye sons of men?
　Nay, rather in your hearts
　　Ye ponder wickedness,

And violence ye deal throughout the land:
Even from the womb the wicked go astray,
　Even from the birth deceive,
　　And underneath their tongue

Lurks the fell poison of the serpent's fang:
Deaf as the adder they, that stops her ear,
　Nor lists the charmer's voice,
　　Though cunningly he charm.

Break Thou the teeth within their mouths, O God,
Break Thou their lion jaws, O Lord: and like
　The swiftly-gliding stream,
　　So let them pass away.

Shiver their arrows when they bend the bow;
Yea, let them perish like the melting snail,
  Or as the untimely birth
    That looks not on the sun.

Scatter with storm the green and arid wood,
Ere the pots feel the thorns. Thy vengeful stroke
  Beholding with glad heart
    The godly seed shall bathe

Their steps in sinful blood; and men shall say,—
'Truly there is a guerdon for the just,
  Truly there is a God
    That judgeth in the earth.'

PSALM LIX.

From my foemen, O my God,
Lift me to Thine high abode;
From the unholy multitude
Save me, from the men of blood.

Mighty ones in leaguèd strife
Rise against my guiltless life:
Lord, uninjured they combine,
Unprovoked by fault of mine.

Wake, my Helper, and behold
How they muster, strong and bold:
Thou the God of hosts, O Lord,
God of Jacob, our adored,

Wake, we pray Thee; rise and quell
Heathen foes of Israel:
All who league for traitorous war
Strike in judgment, strike, nor spare.

Every eve returning back
Round the city growls the pack,
Merest mischief all their words,
And their tongues are very swords:

'For who hears?'—The heathen's pride,
Lord, Thy scornful eyes deride:
Therefore in my direst strait,
O my Strength, on Thee I wait:

God my fort, the God of love,
Watcheth o'er me from above;
Stricken by His arm I see
Every foe that strikes at me.

Beat them down, but slay not quite,
Lest the tribes forget Thy might;
Lord, our shield, disperse them wide
O'er the earth with bated pride.

For their high and vaunting speech,
For the sinful lore they teach,
For their lies and cursings, Lord,
Ruin be their just reward.

In Thine anger lay them low,
Root them out, that men may know
God in Jacob ruleth still,
Utmost earth obeys His will.

Every eve returning back
Let them growl—the noisy pack:
Round the city let them stray,
Prowl all night, nor find their prey.

Thou shalt be my morning song,
God the merciful and strong:
Thou hast been my lofty tower,
Refuge in my troublous hour.

Yea, the joyful hymn of praise,
O my Strength, to Thee I raise,
Watcher o'er me from above,
God of might and God of love.

PSALM LX.

CAST off by Thee, repulsed, forlorn,
O God, our broken strength we mourn;
Let Thy fierce anger burn no more,
But spare us, pardon, and restore.

Rent by Thy desolating hand,
What dire convulsions shake the land!
Our bastions totter to their fall;
O heal at length the ruined wall.

Thy people have been taught to know
The utmost bitterness of woe,
Alas, and from Thy fury's cup
We drank the wine of trembling up.

But they who come before Thy Face
With reverent fear, and seek Thy grace,
Shall see Thy banner reared on high,
The rallying sign of victory.

Redeem the people of Thy choice,
Who cry to Thee with suppliant voice:—
'Behold, Thy guardian help we crave;
Lift up Thy mighty hand and save.'—

Hark, we are heard: the God of might
Hath spoken from His holy height:
'I triumph; lo, my potent rod
Shall portion Shechem's fruitful sod,

And Succoth's vale my measuring-line;
Manasses, Gilead, shall be mine;
Ephraim the helmet on my brow,
My staff of empire, Judah, thou;

My laver shall be Moab's land;
My shoe flung forth to Edom's hand:
Philistia, lift the servile voice
And bid thy conquering lord rejoice.'—

To arms! but who my march will guide
To the strong city of their pride?
To arms! but who shall bring my band
With rebel Edom hand to hand?

Is not Thy grace for ever gone?
Thou wilt not lead our armies on?
Help us, O God: O God, redress:
For human help is profitless.

Be God upon our side, how bright
Will shine our prowess in the fight!
Be God our champion, He will tread
Victorious on the foeman's head.

PSALM LXI.

Give ear, O God, to my complaint,
   And to my prayer reply:
To Thee, what time my heart is faint,
   From earth's far coasts I cry.

Lead to the rock, upon whose height
  The lowly find repose;
My refuge Thou, my tower of might
  Against assailing foes.

Within Thy tent I fain would dwell
  For ever to endure:
Beneath Thy wings I know full well
  My soul shall rest secure.

My vows, O God, are heard by Thee,
  Nor hast Thou spurned my claim;
The heritage Thou givest me
  Of such as fear Thy Name.

Guard for the King his days; sustain
  His years through many an age,
Enthroned before his God to reign,
  And hold his heritage.

Thy loving mercy day by day,
  Thy truth, his safeguard be:
So shall I hymn Thy Name, and pay
  My constant vows to Thee.

PSALM LXII.

My soul doth only rest on God,
  From Him my saving help is shown:
  He is my rock of strength alone,
My refuge He, my safe abode:
  I shall not greatly be o'erthrown.

How long will ye assault a man?
  As though he were a leaning wall,
  A fence that totters to its fall,
How long his weakness will ye scan,
  And join to crush him, one and all?

Yea, they consult with cruel art
　To thrust him from his stately height:
　In falsehood only they delight,
Bless with their mouth, the while their heart
　Runs o'er with cursing and with spite.

But thou, my soul, repose on God;
　From Him my saving hope is shown:
　He is my rock of strength alone,
My refuge He, my safe abode:
　I shall not ever be o'erthrown.

In God my Saviour I rejoice;
　In God my stronghold I abide;
　In Him, ye people, still confide,
Still lift to Him the suppliant voice,
　Our hope, our guardian, and our guide.

Men lowly-born are merely dust,
　And human grandeur but a lie;
　Yea, lighter all than vanity:
In wrong and rapine put no trust,
　Nor yet on growing wealth rely.

Once God hath spoken; twice I learned
　That unto God belongeth might:
　In mercy, Lord, is Thy delight;
And what reward his works have earned
　Thy laws to every man requite.

PSALM LXIII.

O God, Thou art my God: to Thee
　My soul shall sadly cry,
My thirsty soul, my yearning flesh,
　From a drear land, whose springs are dry.

To gaze upon Thy power, to see
  Thy glorious light, I pine,
As oft in olden days I stood
  Adoring at Thy sacred shrine.

My lips shall praise Thee, for Thy love
  Beyond my life I prize;
To Thee my blessing, while I live,
  To Thee my lifted hands shall rise.

My soul, as with all choicest food,
  Shall still be satisfied
With Thee, and from my joyful lips
  Shall flow Thy praise, a ceaseless tide.

In the night-watches, on my bed
  When I remember Thee,
I think of all Thy saving help,
  Thy love so bountiful to me;

And my rejoicing still I deem
  The shadow of Thy wings;
To Thy right hand upholding still
  My soul for its salvation clings:

For Thou deliverest: all the foes
  Who seek to shed my blood,
Surrendered to the sword, shall be
  The dust of earth, the jackal's food.

The king delighteth him in God:
  Who swear by that great Name
Shall glory in their truth, and put
  The lying lips to endless shame.

PSALM LXIV.

Hear, gracious God, my plaintive cry,
   From dreaded foes defend my life;
Defeat their plotting enmity,
   Their tumult and their strife.

Their cruel tongues they whet like swords,
   And, aimed as arrows from the bow,
They darkly shoot their bitter words,
   To lay the just man low.

Fearless they shoot ere he be ware,
   So proud and strong their evil will:
They commune how to set the snare:
   'Who sees?' they mutter still;

Still, as they frame their wicked spell,
   Their lips run o'er with spiteful glee,
'Our cunning plots are woven well;
   Deep counsellors are we'.

But God hath grasped His shafts of wrath;
   He aims the unexpected blow:
They stumble in their haughty path;
   Their vauntings end in woe.

Who look upon their fate, shall fly;
   And men, amazed with sudden fear,
Shall own the righteous doom, and cry,
   'The work of God is here'.

The meek shall in the Lord rejoice,
   Safe sheltered in His strong abode;
Yea, holy men with heart and voice
   Shall glory in their God.

PSALM LXV.

Thee, O God, we calmly trust,
　Praise in Zion shall be Thine,
All our vows with quittance just
　Rendered at Thy holy shrine.

Hearer Thou of human prayer,
　All shall come to Thee, that live:
Sins too great for us to bear
　Thou shalt pity and forgive.

Happy he whom Thou hast placed
　In Thy courts, a chosen guest:
Let us of Thy fulness taste,
　With Thy temple's joy be blest.

Great, O God, Thy saving grace,
　Wonderful Thy truth is found:
Hope of earth's extremest race,
　Hope of ocean's utmost bound.

Girt with power invincible
　By His strength He roots the hills,
Calms the raging billows' swell,
　And the people's madness stills.

Dwellers of remotest lands
　Watch His signs with fearful eye;
Morn and eve, when He commands,
　Shout in joyous rivalry.

God of goodness, from Thy store
　Earth receives the wealthy rain;
Thy full channels gushing o'er
　Raise for man the needful grain.

Earth by Thy soft dews prepared
  Fills her furrows, smoothes her soil;
And her crops with rich reward
  Bless the labourer's happy toil.

With Thy gifts the year is crowned,
  And Thy chariot-paths on high
Scatter o'er the desert ground
  Drops of fatness, as they fly.

Gladness girds the mountain-height,
  Fleecy fields with gladness ring:
Vales with gleaming harvest white
  Shout for gladness, shout and sing.

PSALM LXVI.

Bless God, ye people of the earth,
  And shout with glad acclaim:
Exalt His praise with holy mirth,
  And glorify His Name.

Say ye to God: 'In deeds of might
  How terrible art Thou:
Beneath Thy power in pale affright
  The quailing foemen bow:

Adoring earth Thy Name shall own.'
  Come see the acts of God,
How dreadful to mankind is shown
  His wonder-working rod.

He turned the ocean into land,
  And through the watery ways
Dry-footed went His chosen band,
  And loud we sang His praise.

His searching eyes are everywhere;
  He rules with endless might;
Among the nations who shall dare
  Rebel against His right?

Praise to our God, ye people, give;
  Proclaim it far and wide;
To God, who bids the soul to live,
  Nor leaves the foot to slide.

For Thou hast proved and purged us well,
  As silver in the fire;
Within the net, O God, we fell,
  And bore Thy straitening ire.

Thou sentest riders o'er our head;
  Through flood and flame we past;
But Thou didst bring us out, and lead
  To homes of wealth at last.

Now to Thy temple I will go,
  And pay the victims there,
The vows I uttered in my woe
  With earnestness of prayer.

To Thee the fatlings of my lambs,
  A rich burnt-offering,
To Thee the savoury smoke of rams,
  With bull and goat, I bring.

Come hear from me, ye holy race
  Who live in God's true fear,
His goodness to my soul; His grace
  And strong salvation hear.

I called on Him; His praise the while
  I sang with mouth unfeigned;
The Lord had stopt His ear, if guile
  Within my heart had reigned:

But God hath hearkened to my cry:
  His mighty Name be blest
Who heard my prayer, whose love was nigh
  To give my spirit rest.

PSALM LXVII.

O GRANT us, God of love,
  The blessings of Thy grace;
Reveal to us from heaven above
  The brightness of Thy face:
So shall Thy way on earth be known,
To all mankind Thy mercy shown.

Thee let the people praise;
  All people unto Thee
Sing praise, O God; the kingdoms raise
  A shout of holy glee:
For Thou shalt judge the world aright,
A ruling and a guiding Light.

Thee for Thy bounteous hand
  Let all the people bless,
O God, who givest to the land
  Its teeming fruitfulness.
Still may Thy favour on us rest,
And earth in fearing God be blest.

PSALM LXVIII. PART I.

God ariseth : at the sight
All His foemen turn to flight ;
Sudden fear and awful shame
Scatter all who hate His Name.

He shall chase them with His breath,
Like the smoke that vanisheth :
God is seen : as wax in fire,
Melt the godless, and expire.

Then the righteous all rejoice,
Then with loud exulting voice
Unto God a song they raise,
Bless His Name, and tell His praise :

' Lo, the Desert-rider ! Haste,
Make a highway through the waste :
Call Him by His Name—the Lord !
Shout afar the gladsome word.

Father of the fatherless,
Swift the widow to redress,
Full of goodness, full of grace,
God is in His holy place.

By the mercy of our God
Outcasts find a sure abode,
Captives unto wealth come out,
While the rebels pine in drought.'

Part II.

When through the dismal waste
The favoured nation past,
  Thy fiery shape, O God, before them rode:
The trembling earth was riven;
The meek adoring heaven
  Stooped to the mighty presence of its God.

Then Sinai shook for dread,
And bowed his hoary head:
  God, Israel's present God, the mountain knew:
Then on Thy chosen race
Was showered Thy plenteous grace:
  Weary and faint they drank Thy freshening dew.

Soon dwelt they in the land,
Where, by Thy guiding hand,
  O God, their many sorrows found repose;
Where, at Thy sign, O Lord,
From myriad voices* poured,
  Frequent and full the choral triumph rose.

Kings with their armies fled,
Dismayed, discomfited;
  And spoil-clad maids at home, the folds between,
Showed like the dove†, whose wing
With silver glittering
  Shoots through its plumes a woof of golden sheen.

---

   * al. 'women's voices'.

  † The simile of the dove is by some referred to the glittering spoils hung up by the returning warriors among the sheepfolds (or troughs). The reference to the apparel of the women seems possible, and more pleasing.

PART III.

OFT as to scatter kings
  The Almighty's anger rose,
The tents of Israel gaily shone,
  Like Salmon's gleaming snows*.

Great Bashan's mount is high;
  But why, ye mountains great,
Hate ye the hill which God hath loved,
  The Lord's eternal seat?

With twice ten thousand cars,
  God's thousands, never told,
The Lord goes up, as from His shrine
  On Sinai's height of old.

Thou hast gone up on high,
  And captive to Thee goes
Captivity; Thou takest gifts,
  Lord God, to dwell with foes†.

The Lord, who day by day
  Our burden bears, we bless;
Bless we the God, whose love is nigh
  To save, when men oppress.

Yea, He, who is our God,
  A saving God is known;
The Lord an issue wins from death
  For them that are His own.

---

* The exact meaning here is very doubtful.
† No passage in the Psalms is more difficult than this. See Preface.

But God shall wound the head
  Of all His stubborn foes,
The scalp of him, who, sinning on,
  Nor shame nor sorrow knows.

'I bring thee back, as once
  From Bashan's conquered steep,'
Thus saith the Lord: 'I bring thee back,
  As from the cloven deep:

The victor's lot is thine,
  To dash thy foot in blood,
And from the slaughtered foe to give
  Thy red-tongued hounds their food.'

Part IV.

To the holy place Thy pomp goes past,
  The glorious pomp of my God and King:
The singers are first, the minstrels last,
  And girls in the midst the timbrels ring.
Bless God the Lord on His sacred mount,
All ye tribes that flow from Israel's fount.

There is Benjamin, their ruler small,
  There are Judah's council trooping by:
There are Zebulon's bold captains all,
  And the prudent chiefs of Naphtali.
All our gifts of strength to God belong:
Thou dost work for us: O God, be strong.

For Thy temple's sake on Salem's height
  Wealthy kings with gifts Thy rule shall own:
The beast of the reeds, the bulls of might,
  With the multitude of calves, beat down:

They shall pay to Thee the silver bar:—
He hath crushed the folk that dote on war.

Hither Egypt brings her men of worth;
  Unto God will Cush outstretch her hands:
Sing to God, ye kingdoms of the earth,
  To the Lord sing praises, all ye lands:
From of old He rides the heavens on high,
And His cry is heard, a mighty cry.

Glory to God, our God adored,
  Whose strength is shown in the clouds above:
Thou art dreadful from Thy shrine, O Lord,
  And o'er Israel broods Thy watchful love.
From God are His people's strength and might:
Give praise to God in His holy height.

PSALM LXIX. PART I.

SAVE me, O God; the dangerous billows roll
    About my soul:
In the deep mire I sink, wherein is found
    No standing-ground:

I am come into the depths, and over me
    Sweeps the strong sea.
My cries have wearied me: my throat is dry,
    And fails mine eye;

So earnestly my waiting heart abode
    In prayer to God.
Lo, they that watch my steps with causeless hate,
    Their host how great,

More than the hairs upon my head, and they
    Who seek to slay,
The lying foes who war against my right,—
    What men of might!

I yield what ne'er was won by lawless hand
    To their demand.
O God, Thou knowest my sins; plain to Thine eyes
    My trespass lies.

Lord God of hosts, the men who trust Thy Name
    I would not shame;
Let not Thy saints, O God of Israel, see
    Reproach through me.

For Thy dear sake alone I bear disgrace;
    Shame hides my face;
A stranger to my brethren I am grown,
    A man unknown

To my own mother's children: for the shrine
    Of power divine
My zeal consumes me: daily have I borne
    Thy scorner's scorn:

My tears of penitence, my fasting-times
    Are made my crimes:
I put on sackcloth, and their bitter jeers
    Infest mine ears:

My woes provoke the idler's railing tongue,
    The drunkard's song.
But Thou art ever nigh to guard the just,
    O Lord, my trust.

Part II.

O God, in Thine accepted day
   My prayer is heard above;
Thy pitying mercy now display,
   Thy saving truth and love.

My feet are struggling in the mire;
   Put forth Thine arm, and save:
Preserve me from the foeman's ire,
   And from the whelming wave.

The hungry deep, the wasteful flood,
   The gaping pit control:
Answer, O Lord; as Thou art good,
   Be gracious to my soul.

Hide not Thy face away, but look
   Upon Thy servant's woes;
Draw nigh, redeem my life; rebuke
   My persecuting foes.

My shame and foul dishonour stand
   Unveiled before Thine eyes,
And numbered on Thy truthful hand
   Are all mine enemies.

Reproach hath crushed my heart: with grief
   Outworn and sickening pain
I wait for pity and relief,
   But ever wait in vain:

No friend is nigh with comfort's spell
   To charm away my care;
They give me gall to eat, they quell
   My thirst with vinegar.

Part III.

Let their table be a snare,
Let their wealth entrap their feet,
Sightless make their darkened eyes,
And their trembling backs oppress.

Let Thy wrath upon them glare;
Scorch them with Thy fury's heat;
Roofless may their dwellings rise,
And their homes be tenantless.

For the smitten of Thy hand
They with cruel mockery chase,
Twitting every wounded soul
With the anguish of Thy thrust.

Sin to sin, by Thy command,
Let them add, nor see Thy grace:
Blot them from Thy living roll,
Nor inscribe them with the just.

Part IV.

With weary care brought low
  To Thee, O God, I cry;
Thy saving love shall ease my woe,
  And set my foot on high.

Then will I bless the Name
  Of God with thankful praise,
Then will I magnify His fame
  With loud adoring lays.

Such sacrifice sincere
  Before the Lord is borne,
Than bull more grateful, yea, than steer
  With hoof and sprouting horn.

This shall the meek behold,
  And bless the cheerful sight:
God-seeking hearts shall be consoled,
  And live to fresh delight.

The Lord is swift to hear
  The needy's sad complaints,
Nor doth His eye disdain to cheer
  The bondage of His saints.

His praise let heaven begin;
  Him let the jocund earth,
The seas, and all that move therein,
  Extol with holy mirth.

For Zion God will save,
  And Judah's walls restore,
Where those who love His Name shall have
  A rest for evermore.

PSALM LXX.

Appear, O God, with saving might,
  Be swift to help me, Lord;
With shame and dire confusion smite
  The fierce pursuing horde.

Hurl back my foes in headlong rout,
  And quell their cruel strife,
'Aha, aha,' who rudely shout,
  And hunt my guiltless life.

So shall Thy saints rejoice in Thee,
  Their Saviour loved and tried,
And ever cry with holy glee,
  'Let God be magnified.'

But I am poor and weak, O God;
  Thou guardian of my lot,
My champion strong, with saving rod
  Appear, and tarry not.

PSALM LXXI.

My refuge is Thy holy Name:
Lord, let me never come to shame;
But save me in Thy righteousness,
Incline Thine ear, redeem, and bless.

Be Thou my never-failing fort,
My home of rest, my sure resort:
Thou art my plighted help of yore,
My rock of strength for evermore.

Defend me from the godless foe;
Shield from the smiter's cruel blow;
O Lord my God, from earliest youth
My hope has been Thy stedfast truth.

On Thee my new-born weakness leaned;
Thee, from my mother's bosom weaned,
I followed still: of only Thee
My ever-sounding praise shall be.

While crowds aghast behold my woes,
I look to Thee, and find repose:
Thy Name alone is on my tongue,
Thy glory claims my daily song.

Be with me too in later days,
When eyes grow dim and strength decays:
Still guide my steps, still guard my lot:
In life's last stage forsake me not.

My ruthless foes against me speak;
My life the busy plotters seek:
'Forsaken of his God,' they cry,
'Seize, slay him quick: no aid is nigh.'

Haste Thee to help, O God: control
The furious haters of my soul:
Who plot my fall, confound, consume;
Let shame and ruin be their doom.

So shall I still in Thee confide:
So shall Thy praise be multiplied:
Thy saving truth my mouth shall bless,
Thy mercies vast and numberless.

O Lord my God, Thy might alone,
Thy righteous acts my song shall own:
Those acts my childhood learned from Thee,
And men have heard them, told by me.

In age, O God, and hoary hair
Forsake me not, till I declare
To other times Thy power and grace,
Thy greatness to the coming race.

High as the highest heaven above,
Extends, O God, Thy righteous love;
Whom shall we liken unto Thee,
O God, who workest wondrously?

Thy hand, which dealt me woe and pain,
Now turns to quicken me again:
Yea, to a new and brighter birth
It lifts me from the depths of earth.

By Thee once more with honour blest,
In Thee once more I sweetly rest:
My lute Thy glory shall proclaim,
And chant, O God, Thy faithful Name.

My ringing harp Thy praise shall swell,
Thou Holy One of Israel:
My lips shall shout their loudest glee,
My soul shall sing, redeemed by Thee.

Thy truth my tongue shall ever bless,
And blazon all Thy faithfulness,
Whose arm has scared my blushing foes,
And given my hunted life repose.

PSALM LXXII. PART I.

O GOD, whose gifts alone can bless,
Thy judgments let the King possess;
Give the King's Son Thy righteousness.

His word shall judge Thy nation well,
His doom the sorrows shall dispel
Of such as mourn in Israel.

Rest for the people shall be shed
From every mountain's shining head,
And o'er the hills by truth be spread.

For He shall end the poor man's woes,
Win for the sons of want repose,
And crush their persecuting foes.

Thee with the sunlight men shall fear,
Beneath the nightly moon's career,
While year shall tread on flying year.

He shall come down upon the plain,
As on the mown grass drops the rain,
As showers that water herb and grain.

The just shall flourish in His day,
And peace shall rule with ample sway,
Even till the moon shall fade away.

From sea to sea His reign extends,
From where the River's flood descends
Commencing, with the earth it ends.

His power the desert tribes shall own;
His foes with humbled faces prone
Shall lick the dust before His throne.

Great princes many an offering
From Tarshish and the Isles shall bring,
And Sheba's chiefs and Saba's king.

PART II.

EVERY king shall bow before Him,
Every heathen race adore Him;
   He, the champion of the weak,
Hears the cry of tribulation,
To the friendless brings salvation,
   Spares the needy, guards the meek.

He redeems the souls that languish
In oppression, woe, and anguish;
   Dear their blood is in His sight:

So they live, to Him repaying
Sheba's gold, and, for Him praying,
  Day by day extol His might.

Fed by never-failing fountains
Corn shall rustle on the mountains
  Like the leaves of Lebanon:
As the grass which dew-drops nourish,
In the cities men shall flourish,
  Sire bequeathing joy to son.

Praise to Him the world shall render
Long as suns shall rise in splendour;
  Evermore endures His Name.
Glad shall be His saints, possessing
In His rule their choicest blessing:
  Utmost lands shall tell His fame.

Be the Lord our God confessèd
Israel's God, for ever blessèd;
  Wondrous works alone He shows:
Earth shall sound His famous story,
Earth, o'erflowing with His glory:—
  Loud Amens the service close.

PSALM LXXIII.

God only favours Israel:
The pure in heart He loveth well.
Yet I had nearly gone astray,
My steps had swerved from wisdom's way:

For flourishing in high success
I saw the sons of wickedness,
The men of proud and reckless mind;
And my pale heart with envy pined.

Death cannot bind them: strong and sleek,
The glow of health is on their cheek:
No mortal cares disturb their lot,
Their neighbour's sorrows touch them not:

Thus pride invests them, like a chain,
And, as a mantle, fierce disdain:
Their eyes are full of lustful fires,
And boundless are their heart's desires:

Oppressive are their words and high,
They scoff and speak iniquity:
Their mouth in heaven assumes to reign,
And earth is made their tongue's domain:

And so to them the people bow,
And profits in their channel flow.
How knoweth God? they boldly cry:
What knowledge hath the Lord most High?

Such are the wicked: they have peace,
And wealth in ever large increase.
Ah, then in vain my heart I cleanse,
And wash my hands in innocence:

I wander anguished and forlorn
All day, and chastened every morn.
Yet should I say, 'My lips shall tell
These bitter truths to Israel,'

This were to lead Thy sons astray,
This were to walk the traitor's way.
How may the mortal hope to find
The meaning of the Eternal Mind?

O parable too hard for me!
In vain I strove its scope to see,
Until, God's holy shrine within,
I marked the latter end of sin:

The sinner, lured to slippery ways,
On ruin's brink securely strays,
Till falls the whelming bolt of fate,
And stunned he lies, and desolate.

The pride of sin, if God arise,
Shows like a dream to waking eyes;
The shadow flies, contemned by Thee,
And nought is left but vanity.

Yet oft my chafing thoughts would scan
The wrongs of earth, the woes of man,
So dull, so senseless was my mind,
To Thee, and Thy deep wisdom, blind.

But still Thy goodness kept me Thine;
My hand is in the Hand divine:
Thy counsels lead me, till I see
Thy glorious face, and rest with Thee.

Whom else could heaven itself provide?
What firmer friend, what surer guide?
And, if for love on earth I pine,
What earthly love can equal Thine?

The flesh may sink, the heart may quail,
I trust in that which cannot fail:
My rock of strength, a safe abode,
My portion evermore, is God.

They perish all, whose senseless pride
Turns from Thy saving love aside;
Thy wrath destroys the fools who flee
To base idolatries from Thee.

Nearest to Thee, my God, is best:
In God the Lord my hope I rest,
And ever to the world proclaim
The wonders of His mighty Name.

PSALM LXXIV.

WILT Thou reject us evermore,
  O God? and shall Thy fury rage
Against Thy pasture-sheep of yore,
  Thine own, Thy purchased heritage?
O think upon Thy people still:
Remember Zion's once-loved hill.

Lift up Thy feet: defaced, defiled
  By ruthless foes Thy temple view:
Rings through Thy courts the revel wild
  And shouting of the unholy crew;
Whilst o'er the ruined walls on high
Their conquering standards proudly fly.

Fast as a tangled forest falls
  Beneath the hewing woodman's sway,
The fretwork of Thy gorgeous halls
  Their bars and hammers rend away:
Their impious wrath with heathen flame
Pollutes the dwelling of Thy Name.

'Destroy'—they mutter in their ire,—
  'Destroy for ever all their shrines.'
Our holy spots they waste with fire:
  We see no more our wonted signs:
Amongst us now no prophets dwell,
No tongue, the coming end to tell.

How long shall foemen work their will,
  And mock Thy Name? O God, how long?
Why rests within Thy bosom still
  Thy right-hand terrible and strong?
Haste, pluck it forth: with sudden doom
Thy fierce insulting foes consume.

And yet my King of old was God:
  He showed His wondrous power to save
Amidst the earth: His potent rod
  A highway through the billows clave:
They sank; their heads were bruised by Thee,
The dragon monsters of the sea.

By Thee that tyrant of the flood,
  The myriad-headed crocodile,
Lay crushed and floating many a rood,
  The desert-dweller's banquet vile.
Thou smotest rocks; out leapt the tide:
Thou spakest; mighty streams were dried.

Thou art the Author of the day,
  And Thou the Framer of the night:
Thy works they are, Thy will obey,
  The sun, and every lesser light.
By Thee the bounds of earth were laid:
Summer and winter Thou hast made.

O lay to heart Thy righteous cause:
  Presumptuous foes the Lord gainsay:
A godless nation spurns Thy laws:
  O scare the spoiler from his prey;
Be mindful of Thy former love,
And save Thy perilled turtle-dove.

Thine ancient covenant bring to mind,
  And muse upon Thy plighted grace:
The earth is dark, its dwellers blind,
  A cruel and a lawless race.
O guard the injured soul from shame:
Let the meek mourner praise Thy Name.

Arise, O God, Thy war to wage;
  Let scoffing fools their madness rue:
Forget no more the scorner's rage,
  The roaring of the hostile crew:
For loud and ever louder grows
The tumult of Thy frantic foes.

PSALM LXXV.

WE praise Thee, yea, O God, we praise:
  Thy Name is ever near:
Thy miracles of ancient days
  We tell, that men may fear.

'A day of righteous doom is nigh,'
  Saith God, 'when earth shall fade
With all that dwell therein; yet I—
  Its pillars I have weighed.

Oft to the scornful have I cried,
  Refrain your bitter scorn:
Oft to the sons of impious pride,
  Uplift ye not your horn:

Uplift ye not your horn on high,
  Nor insolently speak
With neck elate and swelling eye
  Against the just and meek.

Not from the day-star's rising light,
  Not from his going down,
Not from the desert mountain-height
  Salvation's strength is shown.

God judgeth by His ruling Word,
  And one He setteth up,
And one He casteth down: the Lord
  Hath in His Hand a cup:

With wine and mingled drink it foams;
  He pours it out on high:
The wicked of the earth He dooms
  To drain it utterly.'

Of Jacob's God my mouth shall tell,
  And sing His endless praise:
The sinner's horn my power shall quell,
  The good man's honour raise.

PSALM LXXVI.

God in Judah's homes is known,
Great in Israel His renown:
Salem was the tent divine,
Zion's height His holy shrine.

There the flaming shafts He broke,
Shield and sword and battle-stroke.
Great art Thou, more glorious far·
Than the spoiler's hill-forts are.

Lapt in dreamless slumber lie
All the hearts of courage high:
Powerless for the morrow's fight
Droop the hands of warring might.

God of Jacob, Thy behest
Steed and chariot lulls to rest:
Awful in Thy strength art Thou:
Who can face Thy glooming brow?

Earth in horror mute and still
Heard from heaven Thy spoken will,
When, to end the mourner's woes,
God, the Judge of men, arose.

Human wrath and hostile spite
Magnify Thy conquering might.
To the Lord your God be paid,
Ye His saints, the vows ye made:

Royal gifts to God belong:
God, the terrible and strong,
God, who curbs the princely head,
Kings of earth behold and dread.

PSALM LXXVII.

My voice to God ascends on high;
To God I lift my earnest cry:
O hearken to my litany.

I seek the Lord in time of dread,
My hands hang open on my bed,
My soul will not be comforted.

I think of God and make my moan;
With fainting heart I muse alone,
Sleep from my painful eyelids flown.

Through weary watches of the night
Thou hold'st mine eyes: in speechless fright
I lie and wait the lingering light.

I call to mind the bygone days,
My nightly song of prayer and praise;
My heart explores Thy secret ways.

Am I cast off for evermore?
Hath God renounced the love He bore,
The favour shown to me of yore?

His promise—doth it cease to bind?
Hath God forgotten to be kind?
Is wrath awake, and mercy blind?

And ah, this woe of mine, I thought,
The will of the Most High hath wrought,
The years of His right hand have brought.

I muse upon Thine ancient praise,
Thy marvels done in olden days,
O Lord, reviewing all Thy ways.

Holy art Thou: what god may be
For mighty works compared with Thee,
O God who doest wondrously?

The nations felt the dreadful stroke,
When Jacob's chain Thy strong arm broke,
And rescued Joseph from the yoke.

The waters saw Thee, God of might,
The waters trembled at the sight,
The sea-caves shuddered with affright.

Amidst the sky's tempestuous wail
Flashed through the gloom Thy fiery hail,
Thy thunder-voice was on the gale:

Earth started at Thy lightning's ray,
Thy march through rolling ocean lay,
O'er mountain-waves Thy wondrous way:

No eye Thy printless footsteps scanned;
Thy flock Thou ledst from land to land
By Moses' staff and Aaron's hand.

PSALM LXXVIII.

My doctrine, O my people, hear,
And to my words incline your ear.
Dark sayings shall my mouth unfold,
And utter parables of old;
Truths which, from earliest ages heard,
In trust to us our sires transferred,
We to our offspring will make known,
That future men the Lord may own,
And tell His wondrous deeds of yore,
And praise His might for evermore.
His testimony Jacob saw;
To Israel's race He gave a law,
Which son from sire should learn to heed,
And seed proclaim to coming seed,
That all, in God confiding still,
Might know His works and keep His will;
Unlike the fathers of their line,
Who, rebels to the Law divine,
Turned from His voice their stubborn ear,
Nor sought His love, nor owned His fear;

As Ephraim's children, armed for war,
Unbent their bows and fled afar.
God's holy covenant they forsook,
His guiding law they would not brook;
His works of wonder they forgot,
His mighty portents heeded not.
He to their sires His power revealed
In Egypt's land, in Zoan's field:
He led them through the cloven deep,
And piled on high a watery heap:
He guided as a cloud by day,
And lit with fire their nightly way:
The desert rock for them He clave,
And drink, as from an ocean, gave;
Forth from the stone a fount it leapt,
And o'er the plain, a river, swept.
Yet sinned they in the desert path,
And goaded the Most High to wrath:
Yea in their heart they tempted God;
Their lust desired a daintier food:
'Can God provide', they dared to say,
'And in the wild a table lay?
He smote the rock, the waters came;
We saw the plenteous flowing stream:
But can He give us bread to eat,
And flesh to be our daily meat?'
This heard the Lord; on Jacob fell
His wrath, and fire on Israel,
Because they turned from God aside,
Nor on His guardian help relied.
The yielding clouds were backward driven,
He oped the mighty gates of heaven;
The nutrient manna rained He down,
And heavenly bread was round them strown:

From angel tables stintless food
Relieved the craving multitude.
He drove the east-wind through the sky,
And bade the wingèd south-wind fly:
Flesh on the camp, as dust, was shed,
And fowls, like countless sea-sand spread,
Fell thick amid their crowded tents,
And clustered round their settlements.
So ate they, and were satisfied;
Their heart's desire was not denied.
Fed to the full, the lustful throng
Were lingering o'er their banquet long,
When rose the sudden wrath of God,
And, smitten by His vengeful rod,
The goodliest of their army died,
The flower of Jacob, Israel's pride.
Such signs they saw, but saw in vain,
Their faithless tempers sinned again.
For this their days in dreams were spent,
Their anxious years in terror went.
They sought Him quickly, when He slew,
And to their God returned anew:
'God is our rock', was then their cry,
'Our Saviour is the God most High.'
So spake the double-minded throng,
So lied to God with flattering tongue;
But still their heart His Name forgot:
His holy Law they valued not.
They sinned, yet God forbore to kill,
His goodness spared and pardoned still.
Oft would He turn away His ire,
And damp His fury's waxing fire:
He knew them flesh, He saw them frail,
And fleeting as the transient gale.

Oft, as the weary waste they trod,
Their crimes provoked the wrath of God;
Once and again their King they tried,
And Israel's Holy One defied.
They mused not on His saving Hand,
Which led them from the foeman's land
His signs when frighted Egypt saw,
And Zoan's field with silent awe
Beheld the river changed to gore,
Till mortal lip could drink no more;
When flies from heaven their land despoiled,
And loathsome frogs their dwellings soiled;
When caterpillars gnawed their shoots,
And locusts ate their tender fruits;
Their vines by hail were beaten down,
By hail their fig-trees overthrown;
Their cattle felt the storm divine,
The blasting lightning slew their kine;
What time to plague His heathen foes
The fiery wrath of God arose
With pains and pangs and troublous fears,
A band of evil messengers:
When for His ire He made a path,
And smote the Egyptian in His wrath,
Spared not from death his proud offence,
But gave him to the pestilence:
When Egypt's first-born He laid low,
And filled the tents of Ham with woe.
His people forth, like sheep, He led:
Safe through the waste and free from dread
He brought them; but the wild sea-wave
Became the chasing foeman's grave.
He brought them to His holy land,
This mount, the purchase of His Hand;

Gave them the soil by line and lot,
Before their face the heathen smote,
And in their conquered tents to dwell
He placed the tribes of Israel.
Yet the Most High provoked they still,
And would not keep His righteous will:
Still, as their sires, in faithless pride
They turned, like swerving bows, aside.
Their hill-shrines God in anger sees,
And hates their graven images:
God sees, and straight His wrath was shed
Upon estrangèd Israel's head:
He left His home in Shiloh then,
The tent in which He dwelt with men;
His glory once, His ark of might,
He made the spoil of hostile spite.
Wroth with His heritage, He gave
His people to the foeman's glaive:
His young men perished in the fire,
His maidens heard no bridal quire;
Fell by the sword His priestly train,
Nor widow lived to weep the slain.
Yet, as from sleep, awoke the Lord,
As warrior strong by wine restored:
Full on the foes His vengeance came,
And hurled them back with endless shame.
The tents of Joseph pleased not Him,
Nor yet the homes of Ephraim;
In Judah's tribe He chose to rest,
Mount Zion, which He loves the best.
Firm as the heaven His shrine He planned,
Strong as the earth, for aye to stand.
A shepherd youth He deigned to chuse,
David, who watched the teeming ewes,

And bade him rule His people well,
And feed His chosen Israel.
With upright heart he ruled the land,
And fed them with a prudent hand.

PSALM LXXIX.

Behold Thy plundered heritage,
   Thy holy shrine defaced;
Behold, O God, by heathen rage
   Jerusalem laid waste.

Thy slaughtered saints are flung away
   To fowls of heaven for food,
Thy pious worshippers a prey
   To wild beasts of the wood.

Around the city far and wide
   Their blood, like rain, is shed;
Unsepulchred on every side
   We view the ghastly dead.

With men, who jest upon our woes,
   Unhonoured and forlorn
We dwell, and to our bitter foes
   A laughing-stock and scorn.

And must we, Lord, for ever feel
   Thine unappeasèd ire?
And burns Thy jealous fury still,
   A never-ending fire?

On realms that own Thee not be hurled
   Thy fierce avenging flame;
Upon the nations of the world,
   That call not on Thy Name.

Jacob is spoiled; his tents lie waste;
  O Lord, our sins of yore
Remember not; our errors past
  Call Thou to mind no more:

Soon may Thy tender love awake,
  For weak and low are we:
O help, and for Thy glory's sake
  Our God and Saviour be.

Save us, and put our sins away,
  As Thou art good and just,
Nor let the scornful heathen say,
  'Where now the God they trust?'

Avenger of Thy people's blood,
  Before our gladdened eyes
Defeat the godless multitude,
  And hear the captive's sighs;

Redeem the souls condemned to die,
  O Lord: the railing spite
Of neighbours, who Thy truth belie,
  With sevenfold doom requite:

That we, Thy chosen heritage,
  Thy pasture-sheep of yore,
May tell Thy fame from age to age,
  And praise Thee evermore.

PSALM LXXX.

SHEPHERD of Israel, Thou
Who leadest Joseph as a flock, give ear;
  O thronèd on the cherubim,
  Shine forth in sight of Ephraim,

Thy strength unto Manasses show,
In aid of Benjamin appear.
O God, Thy guiding help we crave;
Look on us with Thy radiant face, and save.

Lord God of hosts, how long
Wilt Thou be hot against Thy people's prayer?
Tears are the bread we gain from Thee,
And tears we drink abundantly,
A strife to those we dwell among,
The foeman's jest:—such doom we bear.
O God of hosts, Thy grace we crave,
Look on us with Thy radiant face, and save.

From Egypt brought, a vine
Thou plantedst in the uprooted heathen's ground:
For this an ample room was planned;
It struck its roots, it filled the land;
Crept o'er the hills its leafy bine,
And curled the mighty cedars round:
Unto the sea its boughs were spread,
Its branches to the River's eastern bed.

Why hast Thou rent its fold,
That every passer spoils this plant of Thine?
The forest boar devours its fruits,
The cattle browse upon its shoots:
Turn yet, O God of hosts, behold
From heaven, and visit this Thy vine:
Sustain Thine own implanted tree,
The Son of Thy right hand, made strong for
  Thee.

Cut down, it feeds the flame;
So perish, who Thy frowning visage see.
Let Thy right hand protect its Son,
The Son of Man, Thy strengthened One.

O quicken us, to bless Thy Name;
So shall we not go back from Thee.
Lord God of hosts, Thy grace we crave:
Look on us with Thy radiant face, and save.

PSALM LXXXI.

SING ye aloud to God, our saving strength,
To Jacob's God shout gladly; chant the psalm,
    Bring forth the timbrel, strike
      The pleasant harp and lute.

Blow ye the trumpet at the stated time,
At the new moon, upon our solemn feast;
    A law to Israel this,
      By Jacob's God ordained,

To Joseph for a testimony given,
When God against the land of Egypt rose,
    Where Israel heard a speech
      He did not understand.

'His shoulder from the burden I withdrew,
And from the paniers were his hands relieved:
    When thou in troublous time
      Didst call, I rescued thee.

My answer reached thee from the thunder-cloud;
I proved thee at the fount of Meribah:
    "Hear, O My people, now
      The warning of your God;

O Israel, wouldst thou hearken unto Me!
Be no strange worship thine, nor bow thee down
    To any stranger's god:
      The Lord thy God am I,

Who brought thee forth from Egypt's tyrant land:
Ope wide thy mouth, and I will fill it full."
 But to My warning voice
  My people hearkened not,
And Israel was not willing to obey:
So did I yield them to their own hard hearts;
 And on they walked, misled
  By counsels of their own.

O that My seed had listened to My voice,
And Israel kept My paths! Full soon My hand
 Had smitten and brought down
  Their proud insulting foes:

The haters of the Lord had crouched, and they
Mine own, had lived for ever, fed by Me
 With finest wheat, and filled
  With honey from the rock.'

PSALM LXXXII.

YE judges of the earth, be still,
While God declares His righteous will:
' How long in your unequal scale
Shall justice lose, and wrong prevail?

Let law the orphan's claim secure:
List to the friendless and the poor:
Protect the weak, assert their right,
And save them from the oppressor's spite.'

Alas, ye neither know nor mark;
Reckless ye wander in the dark,
While earth the dire confusion feels,
And on its deep foundation reels.

Gods ye were named: all lands in you
The children of the Highest knew:
But death your frailty shall betray,
And blend your forms with vulgar clay.

Rise, high-throned God, to vengeance rise;
Redeem the wronged, the proud chastise;
Rule every realm by right divine:
For all the realms of earth are Thine.

PSALM LXXXIII.

O GOD, no more keep silence; be not still;
Hold not Thy peace, O God: for lo, Thy foes
   In tumult rise, and they
     That hate Thee lift the head.

Against Thy people craftily they plot,
And counsel take against Thy treasured ones:
   'Come, let us cut them off;
     A nation let them be

No longer, Israel's name no longer known.'
Such outcry fierce is theirs: with one accord
   Such deep design they lay;
     And leagued against Thee stand

The tents of Edom with the Ishmaelite,
Moab and the Hagarene; to Gebal joined
   Ammon and Amalek;
     The Philistine, with those

Who dwell in wealthy Tyre; with these unites
The Assyrian, succouring the sons of Lot:
   Do Thou to them, as erst
     Thou didst to Midian's band,

As unto Sisera and Jabin's host,
What time they fell near Kishon's brook, what time
   At Endor in the flight
     They fell, and fattened earth.

Make all their chiefs like Oreb and like Zeeb;
As Zebah and Zalmunna be their lords,
   'Seize we for ours'—who shout,—
     'The holy seats of God.'

Drive them like chaff, like stubble, O my God,
Before the wind: as fire the forest rends,
   And as the flame, that sets
     The mountain all ablaze,

So chase them with Thy tempest; with Thy blast
So whelm them; make their faces dark with shame;
   That men may seek Thee, Lord:—
     Confounded evermore

Come they to ruin and a shameful end,
That men may know Thy Name, JEHOVAH, know
   That Thou art the Most High
     Alone o'er all the earth.

PSALM LXXXIV.

O LORD of hosts, my soul cries out,
   How lovely Thine abode!
My pining heart and flesh aspire
   To Thee, the living God.
The sparrow there has found its rest,
And there the swallow builds her nest:
O happy, in Thy courts to dwell,
And evermore Thy praise to tell!

Yea, happy they whose strength Thou art,
  Who seek Thy holy hill,
And, passing through this vale of tears,
  Find springs of comfort still.
From strength to strength they shall proceed:
Their feet to Zion Thou wilt lead,
There to behold, O God, Thy face,
There to enjoy Thine endless grace.

O better than a thousand days
  One day of joy with Thee;
Better to watch Thy doors than dwell
  In homes of luxury!
Lord God of armies, hear our prayer:
O God of Jacob, hear and spare:
On Thine Anointed look, and send
Thy grace to help us and defend.

God is a shield to save, a sun
  To lighten and to bless:
No good will He withhold from them
  Who walk in holiness.
O God of hosts, the mighty Lord,
Blest are the souls that trust Thy word:
Grant us that blessing, Father, Son,
And Holy Spirit, Three in One.

PSALM LXXXV.

Not vain, O Lord, Thy loving word
  Of old to Jacob spoken:
Thy land hath seen its sons restored,
  Their captive fetters broken.

Thy grace hath pardoned all their sin,
  And covered their transgression;
No more in wrath Thy hand will smite,
  Nor yield them to oppression.

For ever shall Thine anger burn,
  And whelm our hearts with sadness?
Turn back, O God our Saviour; turn
  To bring us hope and gladness.
Show us Thy pardoning mercy, Lord,
  And grant us Thy salvation:
Speak peace unto Thy waiting saints,
  And bless Thy chosen nation.

Mine ear shall hearken to the voice
  Of God the Lord most holy;
For He will bid His seed rejoice,
  When they depart from folly.
The Lord's salvation is not far
  From such as truly fear Him:
His glory in our coasts shall dwell,
  And all the world revere Him.

Mercy and truth are one again;
  Peace, righteousness, in union:
Truth rises from the fertile plain,
  Heaven holds with earth communion.
All good to us the Lord shall give;
  Our land its fruits shall render,
And holiness His way prepare
  Who comes our strong defender.

PSALM LXXXVI.

Bow down Thine ear unto my cry;
  In need and sorrow, Lord, I pine:
O God my trust, in love reply;
  Preserve my soul, for I am Thine.

O Lord, be merciful to me;
  All day my prayers before Thee rise:
Refresh Thy servant's soul: to Thee
  On wings of faith, O Lord, it flies.

For Thou art gracious, Thou, to all,
  O Lord, who seek Thee, good and kind;
Then hear, O Lord, my humble call,
  My heart's petition bear in mind.

In troublous time to Thee I groan,
  For Thou wilt hear my voice, O Lord:
Like Thee among the gods is none,
  No marvel like Thy potent Word.

The realms Thou madest, Lord, shall bow
  With praise before Thy glorious throne;
For Thou, O God, art mighty, Thou
  The wonder-working God alone.

Teach me, O Lord, with stedfast aim
  To walk Thy path of righteousness;
Unite my heart to fear Thy Name,
  Inspire my lips that Name to bless.

O Lord my God, eternally
  My whole heart on Thy praise shall dwell;
So boundless was Thy love to me,
  It·saved my soul from nether hell.

The proud, O God, against me stand;
  To slay my soul in fury rise
The men of blood, a lawless band:
  Thy fear is not before their eyes.
But Thou, O Lord, endurest long;
  A God of pity, just and mild;
Then turn to me in love; make strong
  Thy servant; help Thine handmaid's child.
Show me a sign for good, that all
  My haters, Lord, with shame may see
That Thou wast nigh to hear my call,
  To help and guard and comfort me.

PSALM LXXXVII.

UPON the holy hills is His foundation:
  In Zion's gates the Lord delights to dwell
  More than in all the tents of Israel;
City of God, the seat of our salvation,
How rich the splendours of thy coming story!
  Egypt and Babylon, Philistia's coast,
  Tyre, Ethiop lands, enrolled with thee, shall boast
'There each was born'—their people's future glory*.
Birthplace of saints, for so thy name be spoken,
  The Lord most High shall strengthen Zion's might;
  Upon His roll the Lord Himself shall write
'There each was born'—thy children's glorious token.

---

* Another view of this difficult passage is:—Whereas Egypt and other countries register their own citizens, the Lord Himself shall write Zion's children in a roll of His own. This view might be expressed thus:

  Let Egypt, Babylon, Philistia's coast,
    Tyre and the Ethiop realm, with haughty boast,
  'There each was born,' enrol their people's glory. &c.

Hark to the minstrel's strain of exultation!
Hark to the dancers shouting in their glee!
O source of pleasant streams, all hail to thee,
City of God, the seat of our salvation.

PSALM LXXXVIII.

O LORD, the God of my salvation,
  To Thee I cry aloud by day,
  To Thee by night I humbly pray;
Hear Thou my woeful supplication.

My weary soul is full of sadness,
  My life is sinking to the tomb,
  The depths of darkness are my doom,
No strength is left, no gleam of gladness.

Even as the dead, am I discarded;
  As they that slumber in the ground,
  No more in Thy remembrance found,
Nor by Thy guiding hand regarded.

Thou in the nether pit hast bound me,
  In darkness, in the lowest deep;
  Thy stormy surges o'er me sweep,
Thy angry tempest rages round me.

Afar from me my friends are keeping;
  Thou hast made me hateful in their sight;
  I am shut in from morn till night;
Mine eyes decay with endless weeping.

My daily prayers, O Lord, address Thee;
  To Thee my careful hands I spread:
  Wilt Thou work wonders for the dead,
Or shall the buried rise and bless Thee?

Shall the grave speak Thy loving-kindness,
  Thy truth be seen in realms of death,
  Thy marvels in the shade beneath,
Thy mercies in the land of blindness?

I cry to Thee before the morrow,
  And seek, O Lord, Thy help alone;
  My prayer shall come before Thy throne
Each morn, and show Thee all my sorrow.

Ah, why am I so long neglected?
  Why dost Thou hide Thy loving face?
  I pine away without Thy grace,
I perish, Lord, by Thee rejected.

Thy plagues afflict, Thy terrors rend me;
  They compass me, like floods, all day;
  No kind familiar faces stay,
Black darkness only, to befriend me.

PSALM LXXXIX. PART I.

THE loving mercies of the Lord
  My song shall ever praise,
My lips Thy faithfulness record
  To all the coming days.

It stands for evermore, I said,
  The fabric of Thy grace,
And in the highest heaven is laid
  Thy truth's unswerving base.

'I made a covenant with Mine own,
  I sware to My beloved,
That David's seed from David's throne
  Should never be removed.'

PART II.

The heavens declare Thy wondrous fame,
Thy truth the saintly choirs proclaim:
  Where dwells Thy peer, O Lord?
Who sits above the cloudy height,
Who reigns among the sons of light,
  Like Thee to be adored?

God in His holy church is feared,
Above all angel bands revered,
  That round Him sing and shine:
What prince, what mighty ruler boasts
Such power as Thine, Lord God of hosts,
  Such faithfulness as Thine?

Thy strength controls the haughty sea,
Its swelling waves are stilled by Thee:
  Beneath Thy withering blows,
Even as a death-struck warrior prone,
Sank Egypt's pride; o'erwhelmed, o'erthrown
  For ever, sank Thy foes.

Thine are the heavens, the earth is Thine,
The world and all that dwells therein
  By Thee to being came:
The North and South Thy potent voice
Created; Tabor's slopes rejoice,
  And Hermon, in Thy Name.

An arm is Thine of matchless might,
Strong is Thy hand, and in the height
  Thy right hand rules supreme:
Justice and judgment base Thy throne,
Before Thee love and truth flow on
  In everlasting stream.

Happy the people, Lord, who know
The joyful sound, and, as they go,
  Behold Thy guiding face;
With endless joy Thy Name they bless,
While o'er them shines Thy righteousness,
  Thy goodness and Thy grace.

Thou art our high and beauteous tower;
Our horn is lifted by Thy power,
  Strong in Thy strength alone:
For to the Lord belongs our shield,
Our king is he from heaven revealed,
  From Israel's Holy One.

Part III.

Thy voice, O Lord, was manifest from heaven,
  Yea, to Thy chosen Thou didst cry aloud:
'My help unto a warrior I have given,
  A youth, exalted from the vulgar crowd:

My servant David has been found by Me,
  And with My sacred oil his locks are bright:
My guiding Hand along his path shall be,
  My love shall bless him with unconquered might.

His throne no warring tyrant shall o'erthrow,
  No guileful treason shall avail to harm:
Before him I will humble every foe,
  And crush his haters with My smiting arm.

My truth and mercy with him shall reside;
  Uplifted in My Name his horn shall stand;
I bid him hold great ocean's subject tide,
  And grasp the rivers in his strong right hand.

'Thou art my Father,' he shall cry to me,
  'My God, the solid rock of all my power:'
My first-born son, My favoured child is he,
  Among the kings of earth on high to tower.

My mercy shall be his from age to age,
  My covenant ever sure to My beloved;
His sons shall keep their deathless heritage;
  His throne, while heaven abides, shall stand unmoved.'

PART IV.

If his sons forsake My law,
And from My behests withdraw,
If My statutes they profane,
And My rules will not maintain,

Scourged by My chastising rod
They shall mourn the wrath of God.
Yet My mercy shall not die,
Nor My truth will I belie.

Never will I break My oath,
Never change My plighted troth,
Ne'er reverse the doom I swore
By My holy Name of yore:—

'David's seed shall live, his throne
Shine before Me like the sun,
Like the moon, for ever shine,
Like the faithful heavenly sign.'

Part V.

Lord, Thou hast put away Thy darling child;
  Thine own Anointed, by Thy wrath cast down,
Bewails Thy broken plight: with dust defiled
  Low lies his ancient crown.

His bastions all he sees in ruin laid,
  His fences rent by Thee, his folds forlorn,
Robbed by each passer, to his neighbours made
  A byword and a scorn.

Exalted is the right hand of his foes,
  His haters gladdened by Thine angry word:
He wars unblest of Thee; Thy might o'erthrows
  The prowess of his sword.

His throne is prostrate by Thy stern command,
  And shorn the splendour of his former fame;
His youthful days are shortened by Thy hand;
  Thou coverest him with shame.

Part VI.

How long wilt Thou conceal Thy face,
How long, O Lord, withdraw Thy grace?
For ever burns Thy dreadful ire,
A merciless undying fire?

Reflect, how short my vital span;
Why lives in vain Thy creature man?
For where is he who sees not death,
Or from the tomb redeems his breath?

Where are Thy tender mercies gone,
The covenant with Thy chosen One?
Thy early love, Thy faithful word
To David pledged—where are they, Lord?

Remember, Lord, Thy servant's woes;
How many nations are my foes;
How in my bosom I have borne
Their long reproach, their bitter scorn.

Yea, Lord, Thy foes, a scornful crew,
Thine own Anointed's steps pursue.—
Blest be the Lord whom we adore,
Amen, Amen, for evermore.

PSALM XC.

LORD, Thou hast been our dwelling-place
   Through every generation:
Our trust has been Thy saving grace
   In all our tribulation:
Thou, ere the mountains sprang to birth,
Or ever Thou hadst formed the earth,
   Art God from everlasting.

The sons of men return to clay
   When Thou the word hast spoken,
As with a torrent swept away,
   Gone like a vision broken.
A thousand years are in Thy sight
But as a watch within the night,
   Or yesterday departed.

Fair laugh the flowers, whose beauty new
    The dews of morning cherish:
Pale evening comes; with fading hue
    They hang their heads and perish.
So fade we in Thy righteous wrath:
Thine eyes behold our secret path,
    Our deeds and thoughts of evil.

Soon, as a tale, the days are past
    Of those that seem the strongest:
And if to seventy years they last,
    Or fourscore, at the longest,
Labour and sorrow to its close
Reduce our pride. Thy power who knows
    And rightly dreads Thine anger?

O teach us so to count our days,
    That we may use them duly
To guide our heart in wisdom's ways,
    And fear and love Thee truly:
Return, and speak the gladdening word:
With Thy repenting mercy, Lord,
    O satisfy us early.

For long have been our days of pain,
    And long our years of sadness:
To us display Thy grace again,
    And to our sons Thy gladness:
O Lord our God, with favouring love
Shine forth; our handiwork approve,
    And bless our daily labour.

PSALM XCI.

Whoe'er his secret home has made,
  Most High, within Thy citadel,
  His happy lot it is to dwell
At peace beneath the Almighty's shade.

I lift my voice unto the Lord:
  'Thou art my fort, my safe abode;
  My trust I place in Thee, my God,
In Thee, alone to be adored.'—

Yea, from the fowler's deathful lure
  He guards thee, from the noisome pest;
  His mighty wings enfold thee: rest
Beneath those shielding wings secure.

Rest, nor the midnight horror dread,
  Nor arrow flying through the day,
  Nor plague in darkness sent to slay,
Nor fell disease of noontide bred.

Although beside thee thousands fade,
  And myriads at thy right hand die,
  It shall not strike thee: but thine eye
Shall see the sinner's guerdon paid.—

'Thou art, O Lord, my peaceful home.'—
  The Highest is thy sure retreat:
  No ill shall reach thee; to thy seat
No smiting pestilence shall come.

For He shall charge His holy ones
  To keep thee safe in all thy ways:
  Their hands shall bear thee up, and raise
Thy feet above the jarring stones.

Upon the lion thou shalt tread,
  And o'er the rankling adder go;
  The lion's whelp shall feel thy blow,
And thou shalt crush the dragon's head.—

Because he loves Me, let him claim
  My guardian help when harm is nigh:
  For I will set his foot on high,
The man who knows My holy Name.

Oft as he calls on Me in prayer,
  My grace shall answer from above,
  And he shall see My present love
In all his trouble, toil, and care.

My power shall hold him safe, and raise
  His name to honour and renown;
  My saving tenderness shall crown
His life with long and happy days.

PSALM XCII.

How good it is to praise the Lord,
Thy Name, Most Highest, to record,
To tell Thy love at morning light,
Thy faithfulness to listening night,
Inventing thoughtful words to suit
The lyre and harp and ten-stringed lute.

Thy deeds, O Lord, I view with joy,
Thy works my grateful heart employ,
So vast the wonders Thou hast wrought,
So deep to us Thy every thought.
Of this the stupid little wot,
The foolish understand it not.

When, like the grass, the wicked spring,
And evil men are flourishing,
Even then their day of doom impends,
The dreadful day that never ends.
And Thou, the height of height, O Lord.
Alone for ever art adored.

For lo, Thy foes, they fade and fall;
O Lord, Thy scorners perish all.
While from Thy sight in anguish fly
The workers of iniquity,
My horn Thou liftest up to be,
Like the wild bison's, high and free.

Fresh oil anoints me: by Thy grace
I see my foeman's humbled face
With thankful eye; with thankful ear
The wicked traitor's doom I hear.
Like palm-trees tall the righteous show,
Like Lebanon's strong cedars grow;

In the Lord's house they strike their root,
In God's own courts they flower and fruit:
When old, no sapless boughs they shed,
But lifting high the fertile head,
O Lord my rock, Thy truth they prove,
And tell Thy firm unchanging love.

PSALM XCIII.

JEHOVAH reigns, in clothing bright
Of majesty, begirt with might:
  The strong-built earth stands fast,
Thy wondrous work: for evermore
Abides Thy primal throne: of yore
  Thou art, O peerless One, the First, the Last.

The floods, O Lord, uprise; their cry
The floods uplift; and breaking high
   The mighty sea-waves rage:
But high above their noise the Lord
Sits mighty: truth attends Thy Word,
   And holiness Thy house from age to age.

PSALM XCIII. Version II.

The Lord is King: He reigns on high
   In glorious raiment bright;
The Lord is clothed with majesty,
   Begirt with peerless might.

He by His power hath made the world,
   And stablished it so sure,
It may not from its seat be hurled,
   But ever doth endure.

Ere yet this solid earth was wrought,
   Thy throne is set of yore:
Beyond the farthest flight of thought
   Thou art from evermore.

The floods, O Lord, the floods arise:
   With thundering torrent strong
The floods arise, and to the skies
   Uplift their billowy song.

The mighty surge of ocean swells
   And breaks with roaring cry:
But far above its clamour dwells
   The mighty Lord on high.

Through ages past and yet to come
  Abides Thy stable Word:
In holiness Thou hast Thy home,
  O pure and holy Lord.

PSALM XCIV.

SHINE, God of vengeance, shine, O Lord,
  With bright avenging face:
Rise, Judge of earth; with just reward
  Surprise the godless race.

How long shall haughty men bear sway,
  And flaunting vice be strong?
How long shall evil have its way?
  O Lord the Judge, how long?

Thy chosen nation they oppress,
  And smite Thy people, Lord;
The widow and the fatherless
  They slay with murderous sword:

The stranger's life they take; and Thee
  With braggart lips and bold
They spurn: 'Jehovah shall not see,
  Nor Jacob's God behold.'

O foolish seed, O people rude,
  What time will ye discern?
O blind and reckless multitude,
  Begin at length to learn.

The Planter of the ears of men,
  How can He choose but hear?
The eye's Creator—to His ken
  What dark thing is not clear?

Who weighs the nations in His hand,
  Shall He withhold the rod?
Who teacheth men to understand,
  Is He an erring God?

The Lord, who formed the mind, descries
  Its inly-moving springs,
And notes with undeluded eyes
  Man's vain imaginings.

But blest is he, O Lord, whose heart
  Thy chastening holds in awe,
Who learns from Thee the better part,
  To love Thy perfect law.

For Thou wilt give him rest, and guard
  His life in evil days,
Until the pit shall be prepared
  For men of wicked ways.

The Lord will save His own, nor slight
  The nation of His choice:
The righteous shall recover right,
  The meek of heart rejoice.

Who shall arise upon my side
  When banded sinners rage?
Against the daring sons of pride
  My battles who will wage?

But for the Lord, my soul had sought
  Ere now the silent land;
I wavered, but Thy kindness taught
  My sliding feet to stand.

When countless thoughts, a billowy sea,
  Within my bosom roll,
Thy tender mercies visit me,
  Thy comforts ease my soul.

What plight hast Thou with men, whose laws
  Are wickedness and lust,
Who band against the guiltless cause,
  And slay the pure and just?

My trusted fortress is the Lord,
  And God my rock I praise:
The Lord our God with smiting sword
  The sinner's guilt repays.

PSALM XCV.

O COME let us uplift our voice
  And sing unto the Lord,
In His redeeming strength rejoice,
  And bless His saving Word.

Yea, let us stand before His face
  In glad and thankful mood,
And praise Him in His holy place
  With psalms of gratitude.

Unto the Lord who would not sing?
  A mighty God is He;
Above all other gods a King
  Of glorious majesty.

The secrets of the earth so deep,
  The corners of the land,
The heights of mountains huge and steep—
  He holds them in His hand.

The floods of ocean all are His,
  And He prepared their frame;
The earth and all that in it is
  By Him to being came.

Come bow we down and bless the Lord,
  Before His footstool fall,
And worship Him with one accord,
  The Lord who made us all.

Our God, our gracious God is He,
  Who chose us for His own;
His pasture-sheep alone are we,
  Our guide His Hand alone.

This day His voice of warning hear:—
  'O be not hard of heart;
Lest, as your fathers erred, ye err,
  And from My paths depart:

They tried the Lord at Meribah,
  They sinned on Massah's day;
They proved Me still, and still they saw
  My wonders by the way;

They grieved me forty years; and then,
  "A heart" I said "of ill
Is theirs; a race of erring men,
  They have not known My will:"

Till, wrath prevailing against love,
  I sware a stern behest,
That still in exile they should rove,
  Nor come into My rest.'

PSALM XCVI.

Sing a new song unto the Lord,
  Sing to the Lord, O earth:
His Name, alone to be adored,
  Exalt with holy mirth.

His wonders publish day by day,
  Of His salvation boast;
To heathen lands His fame display,
  His might from coast to coast.

High is the Lord, all gods above
  A glorious God declared:
Their idols vain let heathens love;
  Our Lord the heavens prepared.

Honour and majesty before
  His face their march combine,
And strength is seated evermore,
  And beauty, midst His shrine.

Glory and might to Him belong:
  The Lord, ye people, bless;
Extol His Name, His temple throng,
  Arrayed in holiness:

Bring sacrifice and pay the vow:
  Approach His holy place,
O trembling earth, and humbly bow
  Before His awful face.

Tell it abroad among the lands,
  'The Lord is King above:'
And say—'The world so firmly stands,
  That it shall never move.'

He comes to judge, our righteous King:
   Let heaven and earth rejoice;
Let all the wealth of ocean sing
   With full resounding voice:

Aloud let every meadow shout,
   And all its flowery pride;
The giant forest-trees tell out
   Their gladness far and wide:

For lo, He comes, the faithful Lord,
   Earth's sorrows to redress,
And judge the nations with His Word
   Of truth and righteousness.

PSALM XCVII.

THE Lord is King: glad earth, and ye,
   O myriad isles, exult aloud:
   Around Him darkness dwells and cloud;
His throne is laid in equity:
A wasteful flame before Him goes,
And burns up His encircling foes.

His lightnings set the world afire,
   And shuddering earth His shafts appal;
   Before earth's Lord, the Lord of all,
The melting hills, as wax, retire.
His righteousness from heaven is shown;
His glory to all nations known.

Shamed be each idol-worshipper,
   And such as dote on nothingness:
   Him, all ye gods, adore and bless:
Glad Zion shall the tidings hear,
And Judah's daughters shout for joy:
Thy judgments, Lord, their thought employ.

Far o'er the earth, beyond the sky,
  Thou sittest, Lord, the height of height,
  Above all gods supreme in might,
Sublime in awful majesty.
Who love the Lord, depart from ill:
The meek are cherished by Him still:

He saves them from the godless hand:
  Yea, for the pious light is sown,
  And gladness to the upright shown:
Be glad then, O ye saintly band;
Rejoice for ever in the Lord,
For ever praise His holy Word.

PSALM XCVIII.

Sing to the Lord a new-made song:
Great miracles to Him belong:
His right hand and His holy arm are strong.

The Lord revealed His saving might
Before the startled heathen's sight:
His faithfulness shone forth in cloudless light.

To Israel's house His truth is shown,
His love remembered to His own;
Our God's salvation utmost lands have known.

Shout to the Lord, and utter forth
A glorious voice, ye realms of earth;
Break out in song, rejoice with thankful mirth:

Come with the merry harp, and sing;
Bring forth the trump, the clarion bring,
And make glad music to the Lord the King.

Roar, many-voicèd mighty sea;
This world, with all its tenantry:
Let streams clap hands, and mountains blend
    their glee.

For lo, the Lord! He comes to bless
The earth; its sorrows to redress,
And judge its realms with truth and righteousness.

PSALM XCIX.

THE Lord is King: with fear
The restless nations hear;
  Cherub-throned He soareth;
  Quivering earth adoreth:
Great the Lord on Zion's height
Sits supreme in regal might.

They praise Thee, Lord, in song,
The terrible, the strong:
  Holy One they name Thee,
  Righteous King proclaim Thee,
Founded by whose faithful hand
Truth and right in Jacob stand.

The Lord our God extol;
Before His footstool fall
  Praying: He is holy:
  He will hear the lowly:
Moses, Aaron's priestly word,
Samuel's prophet voice, He heard.

Yea, when their faith He saw,
He gave them His true Law,
  All His statutes telling
  From His cloudy dwelling:

Lord, to Thee their faults were owned,
Thee a pardoning God they found:

Yet did their sins provoke
Full oft Thy vengeful stroke.
  God the Lord adore ye;
  In His height of glory
Praise Him: holy His abode,
Holy He, the Lord our God!

PSALM C.

ALL people that on earth do dwell,
  Sing to the Lord with cheerful voice;
Him serve with fear, His praise forth tell,
  Come ye before Him, and rejoice.

The Lord, ye know, is God indeed;
  Without our aid He did us make:
We are His flock, He doth us feed,
  And for His sheep He doth us take.

O enter then His gates with praise,
  Approach with joy His courts unto;
Praise, laud, and bless His Name always,
  For it is seemly so to do.

For why? the Lord our God is good,
  His mercy is for ever sure;
His truth at all times firmly stood,
  And shall from age to age endure.

STERNHOLD AND HOPKINS.

PSALM C.

Sing unto the Lord with mirth,
All ye nations of the earth:
Serve the Lord with holy glee,
Shout before Him joyfully.

Know, the Lord is God alone;
His hand made us, not our own;
We, the people of His love,
Sheep that in His pasture rove.

In His gates thanksgiving raise,
Come into His courts with praise:
Own His kindness, tell His fame;
Laud and bless His glorious Name.

Bless the Lord: for good is He,
Merciful eternally;
And His faithfulness secure
Shall from age to age endure.

PSALM CI.

Lord, Thy love and truth I praise;
  My song shall honour Thee;
I will walk in upright ways;
  When wilt Thou come to me?
In my quiet household still
  With soul sincere I will abide:
To no deed or thought of ill
  My steps shall turn aside.

Sin and sinners I reprove,
  And warn them to depart:
Godless friends I ne'er will love,
  Nor men of froward heart.
Whoso stabs with secret lie
  His neighbour's fame, be death his lot:
Haughty soul and scornful eye,
  I will endure them not.

On the loyal sort I look,
  That with me they may dwell:
Righteous ways who ne'er forsook,
  That man will serve me well.
Crafty counsellors of wrong
  Within my gates shall find no place:
Never shall the glozing tongue
  Be stablished in my grace.

When I rise with morning light,
  And in the judgment stand,
Evil-doers I will smite,
  And root them from the land.
From the city of the Lord
  My sentence shall abolish sin:
Such as hate His holy Word
  Shall have no seat therein.

PSALM CII. PART I.

**The prostrate sufferer's Prayer, outpoured
in plaintive woe before the Lord.**

Lord, hear my prayer, and let my cry
   Find access to Thy throne of grace;
   Hide not from me Thy cheering face
When times are dark and trouble nigh.

O listen kindly when I pray,
   And haste my piteous call to hear:
   My days, as smoke-wreaths, disappear,
As firebrands, waste my bones away.

My heart is like a smitten flower;
   Of daily bread I take no thought:
   My bones, with sickening pain o'erwrought,
Cleave to my flesh, devoid of power.

A pelican in desert rude,
   An owl that ne'er its ruin leaves,
   A mateless sparrow on the eaves—
Like theirs my wakeful solitude.

My foes and furious slanderers
   In restless league against me meet:
   Ashes are all the bread I eat,
And all my drink is mixed with tears.

This is Thy wrath: for Thou, alas,
   Didst lift me up to cast me down:
   My days are as a shadow flown,
And I am withered like the grass.

But Thy great empire has no date:
　From age to age endures Thy strength:
　Arise, O Lord, arise at length,
And pity Zion's rueful state.

Yea, Lord, the time is come to rise,
　The moment to retrieve her right:
　Even in her stones Thy saints delight,
Though mourning in the dust she lies.

Thy Name shall hold the realms in thrall,
　Thy glory kings of earth shall fear;
　For in His glory shall appear
The Lord, restoring Zion's wall.

He hears the sighing of distress,
　Nor spurns the sorrows of the meek;
　This truth to coming ages speak,
That men unborn the Lord may bless.

The Lord looks down from heaven on high;
　Earth from His holy height He sees,
　The captive's groaning fain to ease,
And soothe the pangs of them that die;

That they to Zion may record
　His Name, His praise in Salem's street,
　What time the swarming nations meet,
The kingdoms all, to serve the Lord.

PART II.

I walked the path of life, my strength
　Still weakened by His stern command,
My days still shortened, till at length,
　'My God,' I said, 'refrain Thy hand.'

I said: 'O take me not away
  Ere half my fleeting age is o'er:
But Thou—Thy years shall not decay
  For ever and for evermore.

By Thee of old arose the earth;
  Its deep foundations Thou hast laid:
From Thee the heavens derived their birth,
  Thy skill their mighty fabric made.

They wane, they perish; Thou at rest
  Unscathed abidest, underanged:
They fade like raiment: as a vest
  Thou changest them, and they are changed:

But Thou, the unchanging, Thou art He
  Whose years run on their endless race:
Thy servants' sons shall dwell with Thee,
  Their seed shall stand before Thy face.

PSALM CIII. Part I.

Praise, O my soul, the Lord, and all
  Within me praise His holy Name.
Praise, O my soul, the Lord, recall
  His bounteous gifts, His grace proclaim;

Who deigns to pardon all thy sin,
  Thy sickly frame with health to bless,
Yea, from the grave thy life to win,
  And crown thee with His tenderness;

Who fills thee full with every good,
  And gives thee beauty fresh and fair,
That so thy lusty youth renewed,
  Like the bold eagle, cleaves the air.

The Lord for all who are opprest
  A doom achieves of truth and right,
To Moses made He manifest
  His ways, to Israel's sons His might.

The Lord is kind and rich in love;
  His grace and mercy never die:
He will not to the end reprove,
  Nor keep His wrath eternally.

He hath not dealt our mortal lot
  By penal judgment's strict demand;
The measure of our sin is not
  A law to His benignant hand.

From earth to heaven how vast the space,
  How wide from east the setting day,
To all His saints so large His grace,
  So far He puts our guilt away.

As on his sons a father's heart,
  The Lord hath pity on the just:
He knows our frame in every part,
  He bears in mind that we are dust.

PART II.

THE life of man is like the grass;
His blooming days, as field-flowers, pass:
The north-wind blows; their pride is o'er;
The place that knew them knows no more.
But still the Lord from age to age
Sustains His holy heritage:
His happy saints behold His grace,
His truth their children's latest race,
Who keep His righteous judgments still,
And live obedient to His will.

The Lord in heaven hath set His throne;
He rules o'er all, supreme, alone.
O ye His angels, praise the Lord,
Ye mighty, that fulfil His word:
All ye who listen to His voice,
And in His glorious works rejoice.
Praise ye the Lord, His hosts of light,
Who serve Him in the heavenly height:
Praise ye the Lord from pole to pole,
Bright wanderers. Bless the Lord, my souL

PSALM CIV.

PRAISE, O my soul, the Lord: how great,
    O Lord my God, how bright
In majesty, Thy robe of state,
    And raiment of the light,
Thou sittest, spreading for Thy tent
The curtain of the firmament!

His chamber-beams the waters vast,
    The clouds His chariot form;
He rides upon the wingèd blast,
    And curbs the chafing storm:
The winds, His viewless angels, fly;
His courier lightnings fire the sky.

By Him the earth is strongly laid,
    A fabric ne'er to move;
The floods, a veil of floating shade,
    Hang o'er it from above:
The waters, severed from the land,
High o'er the mountain-summits stand:

Before Thy chiding voice they quail,
  Before Thy thunder flee:
They climb the rock, they throng the vale,
  The place assigned by Thee:
Thy settled bounds they ne'er disdain,
Nor turn to whelm the earth again.

Through deep ravines His fountains burst,
  And glide by every hill:
The forest roamers slake their thirst,
  The wild ass drinks his fill:
And, nestling nigh, the birds of air
Rain from the boughs their love-notes there.

His vaults the fruitful water yield
  Adown the slopes to flow,
And for the cattle of the field
  He makes the grass to grow,
For human tillage bringing grain,
And raising bread-corn from the plain.

His golden summers swell the vine,
  His suns the olive rear,
Man's heart to gladden with His wine,
  Man's face with oil to cheer:
And bread, that forms the sturdy limb,
God sends, to feed and strengthen him.

His trees are watered; cedars strong
  Of Lebanon, His work,
Hold roosting birds, and dwells among
  His cypresses the stork:
The wild-goat haunts the mountain-peak,
Their rocky cells the conies seek.

The moon and sun, whose circuits mark
  The gliding month and day,
Thou madest, and the midnight dark,
  When, roaring for their prey,
Prowl forth the wild-beasts of the wood,
And lions seek from God their food.

Up springs the sun; they shrink again
  And in their dens abide;
Man issues to his labour then,
  And toils till eventide.
Such various works, O Lord, are Thine,
All made in wisdom, all divine.

Nor earth alone His bounties bless;
  In ocean's spacious hall
Dwell moving creatures numberless,
  The mighty with the small:
There go the ships, there revels free
Leviathan, ordained by Thee.

All wait on Thee for meat: all live
  Beneath Thy wise control;
'Tis Thine in season due to give;
  They gather up the dole:
Thy opening hands dispense their food,
And they are satisfied with good.

But lo, Thy face is veiled in shade;
  Their spirits sink with fear:
Thou callest back their breath; they fade
  To dust, and disappear:
Thou breathest, they return to light,
And earth again is new and bright.

The Lord for ever dwell adored
  In glorious majesty,
Glad in His creatures be the Lord!
  Beneath His awful eye
Trembles the earth: the mountain-spire
He touches, and it smokes with fire.

As long as life endures, my tongue
  Unto the Lord shall sing;
While being lasts, my thankful song
  Shall praise my God and King:
So may I please Him with my voice,
So in the Lord shall I rejoice.

But sinners—they shall be consumed:
  The ungodly from the earth
Shall fade, to swift destruction doomed.
  With hymns of holy mirth
Praise, O my soul, His Name; record
His power and glory: praise the Lord.

PSALM CV.

PRAISE ye the Lord and call upon His Name;
Among the nations make His doings known:
  Chant ye to Him a psalm,
    Shew forth His wondrous works.

Still be your boast His holy Name; their hearts
Be glad, who seek the Lord: seek ye the Lord
  And His unconquered might;
    His face for ever seek.

Ye seed of Abraham, His servant old,
Ye sons of Jacob, chosen for His own,
  His marvels call to mind,
    His miracles of yore,

The judgments of His mouth. He is our God,
The Lord! His judgments are in all the earth;
   He ever bears in mind
     His ancient covenant,

The word to countless generations sealed,
The treaty made of old with Abraham,
   The oath to Isaac sworn,
     To Jacob for a law

Confirmed, and for an everlasting plight
To chosen Israel uttered:—'Canaan's land
   I give to be the lot
     Of your inheritance:'—

Few though they were and strangers in the land.
So, while from soil to soil, from realm to realm
   They trod their weary way,
     He let no human hand

Oppress them; for their sake rebuked He kings;
Touch not, He said, Mine own anointed ones,
   Nor venture to afflict
     The prophets of My mouth.

What time He called a famine on the land,
And broke the staff of bread, He sent forth one,
   Joseph, a bondsman sold,
     Whose feet, in iron bound,

They galled with fetters, till in destined time
His saying came to pass, and the Lord's word
   Approved him true: then sent
     The king, and let him loose;

The ruler of the nation set him free:
Chief in his house he made him, lord of all
    His goods, to bind at will
        The princes, and to teach

The elders wisdom. When to Egypt came
Israel, and Jacob in the land of Ham
    A sojourner was seen,
        Then did the Lord increase

His own, and made them stronger than their foes.
But soon He changed the heathen's hearts, to hate
    His people, and to use
        His servants craftily.

Moses He sent and Aaron, chosen men,
Who wrought His miracles among them: signs
    They wrought in Ham: He sent
        Darkness, and it was dark:

And then against His will they strove no more.
He turned their waters into blood; and made
    Their fish to die: their land
        He made with frogs to swarm,

Even in the chambers of their kings. He spake,
And flies came forth, and lice in all their coasts;
    For rain He gave them hail
        With flaming bolts of fire.

He smote their vines and fig-trees, yea, He brake
The trees throughout their land. Again He spake,
    And came the locust, came
        A caterpillar swarm

Unnumbered, gnawing every herb and leaf,
Devouring all their fruit. He likewise smote
   The first-born in their land,
     The prime of all their strength:

His own with gold and silver He brought forth,
No feeble frame among their tribes: they went,
   And Egypt was right glad:
     For on the Egyptian host

A fear of them had fallen. He spread out
A cloud to cover them, and pillared fire
   To light them through the night:
     They asked, and He brought quails,

And filled them also with His bread from heaven.
He oped the rock, and forth the water gushed,
   And, as a river flows,
     So flowed it through the waste.

Well did He bear in mind His holy plight,
And Abraham His servant. So He led
   His people forth with joy,
     His chosen with a song;

And gave them heathen lands in heritage,
To till the conquered glebe; that they might keep
   His statutes, and observe
     His will. The Lord be praised.

PSALM CVI.

PRAISE ye the Lord, aye praise; for He is good:
His grace endures for ever: who shall tell
   His mighty acts, or show
     The fullness of His fame?

Happy the men who walk in equity,
Ne'er swerving from the rule of right. O Lord,
   Think of me with the love
     Thou bearest to Thine own:

Show me Thy saving grace, that I may view
Thy chosen blooming with prosperity;
   That my delighted heart
     May share Thy people's joy,

And with Thine heritage exult. Alas,
We have sinned, as did our fathers; we have dealt
   Perversely, we have walked
     In paths of wickedness.

Our fathers, weighing not Thy wonders done
In Egypt, mindless of Thy plenteous love,
   Rebelled beside the sea,
     Even by the Red sea-wave.

Yet did He save them for His own Name's sake,
That He might make His greatness to be known;
   Yea, to the Red sea-wave
     He spake, and it was dried.

So through the deep, as o'er the desert sands,
He led them; from their fierce pursuing foes
   He kept them safe; their foes
     The waters overwhelmed;

Not one of them survived. His people then
Believed His promises, and sang His praise;
   Yet soon forgot His works,
     Nor waited for His word;

But lusting in the wilderness for meat,
They tempted God. Then granted He their prayer,
   But armed against their lives
     A wasting malady.

They envied Moses, leader of the camp,
And Aaron, holy priest: then yawned the earth
   And, swallowing Dathan up,
     It whelmed Abiram's band.

Against their company blazed forth a fire,
Whose flame burnt up the wicked. Yet a calf
   In Horeb did they make,
     Before a molten god

Bow down, and to the glory of the Lord
Prefer the likeness of a grazing ox.
   Their hearts forgot their God,
     Their Saviour, who had wrought

Such mighty works in Egypt, wondrous deeds
In Ham's inheritance, and fearful things
   Beside the Red sea-wave.
     Then was their angry Lord

Fain to destroy them: but before Him stood
His chosen servant Moses in the breach,
   And turned away His wrath,
     That He destroyed them not.

They spurned the pleasant land, and, trustless to
The Lord's great promise, murmured in their tents,
   Nor hearkened to His voice:
     Then lifting up His hand

He sware that He would cause them in the waste
To die, that He would cast their children forth
    Through heathen lands dispersed
        To serve a godless race.

To Baal-peor's rites they flocked, and ate
A lifeless idol's victims: thus their sin
    Provoked the Lord to wrath,
        And on them broke the plague.

Then stood up Phinehas, and achieved revenge:
And so the pest was stayed: which act to him
    Counts for a righteous act.
        Till time shall be no more.

They vexed Him by the streams of Meribah,
And Moses bore the penal stroke: enraged
    At heart, he rashly spake
        With unadvisèd lips.

The nations they destroyed not, though the Lord
Such order gave: but with the heathen tribes
    Commingling, learned their works,
        Yea, to their idol gods

Did homage; so were these a snare to them:
To demons oft they sacrificed their sons
    And daughters: guiltless blood
        Of daughters and of sons

They shed, to Canaanitish idols slain:
The land was foul with gore; and thus were they
    With evil works defiled
        And base idolatries.

Then the Lord's wrath against His people burned,
And He abhorred His heritage, and soon
    He gave them to the yoke
        Of cruel heathen lords.

Them, by their foes bowed down and sore opprest,
Oft did the Lord deliver ; oft their sins
    Provoked Him yet again
        To smite and bring them low.

Once more He saw their trouble, heard once more
Their cry, and, mindful of His ancient plight,
    In His abundant love
        Relenting from His ire

He made the captives pitied of their lords.
Save us, O Lord our God, and gather us
    From out the heathen lands,
        That we may sing Thy praise

And bless Thy holy Name. Blest be the Lord,
The God of Israel, now and evermore:
    And all the people say
        'Amen, the Lord be praised.'

PSALM CVII.

    Praise ye the Lord, for very good
        And full of grace is He :
    His loving-kindness never fails
        Through all eternity.—

    Be thankful they whose many woes
        The saving Lord redress'd,
    And gathered them from every land,
        North, South, and East and West.

Far in the weary wilderness
  They wandered from the road,
And there no lasting city found,
  No strong and sure abode:

Their soul was drooping in their breast,
  With thirst and hunger faint:
At length they cried unto the Lord,
  And made their sad complaint;

And He redeemed them from their toil,
  And led their wandering feet
Straight to the city of their hope,
  Their everlasting seat.

The goodness of the Lord let these
  Declare with thankful mind,
The wonders that He works to save
  The children of mankind:

The soul that pined in emptiness
  He satisfied with food,
The comfortless and famished soul
  He filled with every good.—

The mourners who in darkness sit
  And in the shade of death,
Fast bound in pain and iron bonds,
  His mercy comforteth.

Rebellious to the words of God,
  The laws of the most High
They proudly spurned, and He brought down
  Their heart with misery:

They fell, and there was none to aid;
 But when their prayer arose,
Their cry of trouble to the Lord,
 He saved them from their woes;

He brought them from the darkness forth
 And from the shade of death;
He brake their iron bonds in twain,
 And eased their failing breath.

The goodness of the Lord let these
 Declare with thankful mind,
The wonders that He works to save .
 The children of mankind:

'Twas He that burst the doors of brass,
 And rent the bar of steel—
Fools for their sin are plagued, the rod
 For their offence they feel:

All food their sickly soul abhors;
 The gates of death are nigh:
Then to the Lord in their distress
 They made a doleful cry:

He heard, and saved them from their strait;
 He sent His word, and healed:
Their soul He rescued from the pit,
 Their doom of death repealed.

The goodness of the Lord let these
 Declare with thankful mind,
The wonders that He works to save
 The children of mankind:

Yea, let them render unto Him
   The sacrifice of praise,
And tell of all His acts, and loud
   Their song of triumph raise.—

Who plough the sea with ships, and fruit
   In many waters reap,
They see the Lord's great works, and note
   His wonders in the deep.

For lo, there rose a stormy wind :
   He spake, and it was still :
The billows swelled and sank again
   By His o'ermastering will.

Now tossing up to heaven, and now
   The hollow floods beneath,
Their troubled heart within them melts
   Upon the brink of death :

They stagger as from wine, they reel
   As men whose wits are fled :
Then cried they to the Lord : He came,
   And they were comforted.

He lulls the storm ; the wave is mute ;
   They rest in glad repose,
And, guided by His love, attain
   The end of all their woes.

The goodness of the Lord let these
   Declare with thankful mind,
The wonders that He works to save
   The children of mankind :

Yea, with the great adoring crowd
  Their Saviour let them praise,
And, where the assembled elders sit,
  The glad thanksgiving raise.—

A land of streams He makes a wild,
  And dries the springs therein;
He turns to salt a fruitful soil,
  To smite the people's sin.

He makes the wilderness a lake,
  The sand a bubbling well;
The hungry build a city there,
  A home wherein to dwell.

He gives large harvests to their field,
  Rich fruitage to their vine;
His blessing multiplies their race,
  Nor lets their cattle pine:

Though long, by stern tyrannic sway
  Diminished and brought low,
They bowed beneath a foreign yoke,
  And bore their silent woe.

In pathless wastes perplexing kings
  He makes their pride a mock;
The poor He saves, and families
  He gives them, like a flock.

The righteous note it, and are glad,
  Sin finds no answering word.—
What wise men know, may all discern,
  The goodness of the Lord!

PSALM CVIII. PART I.

My heart is fain, O God, my heart
  Is fain to sing Thy praise:
My lips shall bear their joyful part,
  And glad thanksgivings raise.

Awake, my glory; with the day,
  Sweet harp and lute, awake;
For I myself will tune my lay
  Ere early morning break.

Among the nations I will bless,
  O Lord, Thy glorious Name;
To utmost lands Thy faithfulness
  In grateful song proclaim.

Thy truth and mercy soar as far
  As highest heaven is high,
Beyond the light of any star
  That glimmers in the sky.

Thy peerless Name be praised, O God,
  Above the cloudy height,
Thy glory told in earth abroad,
  Thy majesty and might.

PART II.

RECEIVE, O God, our suppliant voice,
And aid the people of Thy choice:
Behold, Thy mighty help we crave;
Lift up Thy strong right hand, and save.

Hark, we are heard: the God of might
Hath spoken from His holy height:
'I triumph: lo, My potent rod
Shall portion Shechem's fruitful sod,

And Succoth's vale My measuring-line:
Manasses, Gilead, shall be Mine:
Ephraim the helmet on My brow,
My staff of empire, Judah, thou:

My laver shall be Moab's land;
My shoe flung forth to Edom's hand:
Philistia, thou shalt hear My voice
Within thy conquered streets rejoice.'—

'To arms! but who my march will guide
To the strong city of their pride?
To arms! but who shall bring my band
With rebel Edom hand to hand?'

Is not Thy grace for ever gone?
Thou wilt not lead our armies on?
Help us, O God; O God, redress;
For human help is profitless.

Be God upon our side, how bright
Will shine our prowess in the fight!
Be God our champion, He will tread
Victorious on the foeman's head.

PSALM CIX. Part I.

Hold not Thy peace, O God my praise;
For slanderous tales against me raise
Foul mouths and false: their lips they ope,
And give their lying malice scope.

They compass me with railing spite,
And unassailed against me fight:
My good with evil they repay,
My love with hatred:—I must pray.

'The tyrant o'er him set, the foe
At his right hand: be this his woe:
In judgment let his guilt be shown,
His very prayer as sin set down:

His time on earth a short one make;
His office let another take:
His wife be widowed, and his seed
Beg through the land in orphaned need.

Let strangers prey upon his store,
Seized by the grasping creditor:
No friend, to show him love, be nigh:
His orphans meet no pitying eye.

Let the next age discern no trace
Of all his extirpated race:
The Lord his father's sin repay,
Nor take his mother's guilt away:

Ne'er may the Lord forget their shame,
But tear from earth their hated name.
And why? to need and deep distress
His soul was harsh and merciless:

He vexed the broken heart with strife,
The poor, to take his guiltless life:
Cursing he loved, and such his lot;
Blessing he spurned, and sees it not.

In blasphemy his joy is found,
Even as a robe it wraps him round;
As water down his throat it runs,
Like oil descends into his bones.

And such for ever be the vest
Engirdled round his joyless breast:
Such be the traitor's just reward,
So fare my slanderers from the Lord.'

PART II.

As Thy mercy lasts for ever,
For Thy Name's sake, Lord, deliver
  My distrest and wounded heart:
Lo, with spirits inly pining,
Like a shadow fast declining,
  Like a locust, I depart.

Fasting hath my knees disjointed;
Dim my visage, unanointed;
  Shaken heads my fall proclaim:
As Thy mercy lives for ever,
Me, O Lord my God, deliver
  From reproof and bitter shame.

Be it known Thy hand hath done it;
Thine the victory, Thou hast won it:
  Bless me, though they curse, O Lord;
Crown Thy servant's life with gladness,
Rout and quell their rising madness,
  Clothe with shame the baffled horde.

I will praise the Lord and bless Him,
Loudly to the world confess Him:
  Helper He of want and woe
At the right-hand of the mourner
Stands to save him from the scorner,
  Stands to shame the accusing foe.

PSALM CX.

UNTO my Lord Jehovah said:
  'At My right hand I throne Thee,
Till at Thy feet in triumph laid
  Thy foes their ruler own Thee.'
From Zion hill the Lord shall send
Thy sceptre, till before Thee bend
  The knees of proud rebellion.

Thy saints, to greet Thy day of might,
  In holy raiment muster;
As dew-drops in the morning light
  Thy youths around Thee cluster:
Jehovah swore a firm decree:
'Thou, like Melchizedek, shalt be
  A kingly Priest for ever'.

The Lord at Thy right hand shall bring
  On rulers desolation;
His arm shall smite each heathen king,
  And judge each rebel nation.
He, swiftly marching in His wrath,
Shall quaff the brook upon His path,
  And lift His head in glory.

PSALM CXI.

PRAISE the Lord: with exultation
 Shall my heart His praise proclaim,
In the holy congregation
 Sing thanksgivings to His Name.
Great are all His works, and sought
 By the saints who love His glory,
Musing in their secret thought
 How to spread the wondrous story.

God is good: to them that fear Him
 Tender mercy showing still;
All the righteous, who revere Him,
 Feeding with a constant will.
Mindful of His plighted word,
 And His people failing never,
To their rule doth God accord
 Heathen lands to hold for ever.

Evermore His work abideth,
 Judgment all and verity:
Everything His counsel guideth
 To fulfil His sure decree.
To His saints redemption came,
 As His faithful Word had spoken:
Holy and revered His Name,
 And His covenant stands unbroken.

In the fear of God is grounded
 All the wisdom of the wise:
On this rock securely founded
 Faith believes and hope relies.

Holy Father, praise be Thine;
  Praise, O Son, for Thy salvation:
Holy Spirit, Light divine,
  Sanctify our adoration.

PSALM CXII.

BLEST is the man who fears the Lord,
And truly loves His holy Word:
His seed shall flourish on the earth,
Their offspring happy from the birth.

With riches shall his house abound,
His truth with endless bliss be crowned:
Light dawns in darkness to the kind,
The merciful, the pure in mind.

Blest he who lends with pitying soul:
His house discretion shall control:
No sudden shock shall cast him down,
No time deface his just renown.

No evil rumours shake his breast;
He trusts the Lord, and is at rest,
With fearless heart awaiting still
The fall of those who seek his ill.

His bounty gives to him that needs;
The honour of his righteous deeds
Survives in lasting memory;
His glorious horn ascends on high.

This sinners mark with tortured mind;
For very rage their teeth they grind;
With pining hearts they melt away,
And all their cherished hopes decay.

PSALM CXIII.

O YE who on His service wait,
Praise ye the Lord, for He is great:
　Praise to His Name be given:
From this time forth for evermore,
From east to west His Name adore,
　The Lord of earth and heaven.

Above all nations rules on high
Our God; beyond the starry sky
　His glory far extendeth:
Whom with the Lord will ye compare?
Seated in highest heaven, His care
　To earthly realms descendeth.

He hears the needy when they cry:
He lifts the poor from misery
　To sit in princely places:
To all who want His mercies come,
And oft He fills the childless home
　With children's pleasant faces.

Ye desolate, His aid implore:
Ye saints of God, His grace adore:
　Praise to His Name be given:
Let earth, let heaven's angelic host
Praise Father, Son, and Holy Ghost,
　The God of earth and heaven.

PSALM CXIV.

WHEN Israel came from Egypt's strand,
And Jacob from the stranger's land,
In Judah's camp the Lord abode,
And Israel was the realm of God.

The sea beheld, and shrank with dread;
Back to his fountains Jordan fled:
Bounded the mountain-heights like rams,
The little hills as skipping lambs.

What ails thee that thou fledst, O sea?
Say, Jordan stream, what startled thee?
The mountain-crags what terror thrills?
What quivering shook the lesser hills?

Tremble, thou earth, and quake for fear ·
'Tis Jacob's God :—the Lord is here:
The melting rock obeys His spell:
The flint becomes a springing well.

PSALM CXV.

NOT for our sake—no meed we claim—
  Not for our sake arise, O Lord:
But for the glory of Thy Name,
  Thy goodness, and Thy faithful Word.

Why should the mocking heathen cry,
  'Where now the God they vainly praise?'
Our God enthroned above the sky
  His universe at pleasure sways:

Their idols gold and silver be,
  Wrought by a frail artificer:
Eyes have they, but they cannot see,
  Dumb mouths, and ears that do not hear:

Fools on their altars incense throw,
  Yet smell they none: their hands are bound;
Feet have they, but they cannot go;
  Their throats give passage to no sound:

Mere moulded blocks! yet like to these,
  As senseless all, are they that mould,
Who trust in carvèd images,
  And bow to silver and to gold.

O Israel, be the Lord your guide;
  He is your help, your strong defence:
O Aaron's house, in Him abide,
  Your shield, your stay, your confidence.

The Lord, all ye that fear Him, trust:
  He is your champion in distress:
The Lord is merciful and just
  His faithful worshippers to bless,

To prosper Israel, to create
  New blessings still for Aaron's race,
To help the lowly and the great,
  Who love Him, and await His grace.

A mighty people they shall grow;
  Their children happy from the birth;
Increasing gifts will He bestow,
  Whose power created heaven and earth.

He in the heavenly height resides;
  Supreme o'er all the world He reigns,
And to the sons of men divides
  This earth, and all that it contains.

They praise Him not, the vaults of death,
  Nor can the silent ghosts adore;
Praise we the Lord, who gave us breath,
  Praise we the Lord for evermore.

PSALM CXVI.

I LOVE the Lord; for He is nigh
  My suppliant voice to hear;
To Him shall rise my lifelong cry,
  Who never shuts His ear.
The snares of death, the pains of hell
Drew near; and anguish on me fell.

His Name I called: 'O Lord my trust,
  My captive soul unbind.'
The Lord is merciful and just;
  Our God is very kind.
The Lord preserves the meek: in grief
I languished, and He brought relief.

Return and rest, my soul: the Lord
  Deals bounteously with thee:
For lo, my life from death restored,
  Mine eyes from tears are free,
My feet from falling: I shall stand
Before Him in the living land.

My faith was strong, and so I spake:
  But oft a troubled cry
From out my throbbing bosom brake:
  I murmured, 'All men lie.'
For these His bounties what reward
Shall I present before the Lord?

Be mine from His redeeming hand
  The cup of health to claim,
Amidst His worshippers to stand,
  And bless His holy Name,
My vows unto the Lord to pay,
And with His people sing and pray.

The Lord's compassion values high
   The life-blood of a saint:
Behold, Thy servant, Lord, am I,
   Thine own:—my sad complaint
Thy favour heard; Thy mercy won
From captive bonds Thine handmaid's son.

With thankful sacrifice and song
   I haste to pay my vows
And praise His Name, and with the throng
   That fills His glorious house,
Jerusalem, thy King adored
In thee to worship.—Praise the Lord.

PSALM CXVII.

PRAISE ye the Lord, all nations;
   Ye people, praise the Lord:
For great His loving-kindness,
   And faithful is His Word:

His truth and mercy to us
   Endure for evermore:
Then praise Him, all ye nations,
   O praise Him and adore.

PSALM CXVIII.*

'BLESS ye the Lord, for good is He;
His mercy lives eternally.
Let Israel's strong confession be,
His mercy lives eternally.

---

* This Psalm is said to be a dialogue between a Chorus singing within the temple and worshippers who first ap-

Let Aaron's house repeat with glee,
His mercy lives eternally.
Let them that fear the Lord agree,
His mercy lives eternally.'—

Out of my deep distress I prayed,
And called upon the Lord for aid:
The Lord in kindness heard my cry,
And set my rescued feet on high.

The Lord is with me: shall I view
With terror aught that man can do?
The Lord is on my side: He shows
Beneath me laid my baffled foes.—

'Better to trust the Lord's defence
Than place in men your confidence:
Safer the shadow of His wings
Than all the embattled power of kings.'—

The nations threatened: but the Lord
O'erthrew them by my conquering sword:
Their gathering legions hemmed me round,
But in His Name they bite the ground:

Like bees they came, a countless swarm;
But He upheld my faithful arm,
And lo, they perish in His Name,
As crackling thorns devoured by flame.

proach it from without and then enter. The parts here given to the Chorus stand between *single* inverted commas. The rest belongs to the worshippers. The two lines before the last stanza are spoken by the Chorus to the sacrificing priests.

Ye thrust, to make me fall; in vain:
The Lord was with me, to sustain.
The Lord is still my glorious song,
My Saviour, merciful and strong.

Safe in their tents the godly stand
Rejoicing; "High the Lord's right hand!
The Lord's right hand"—each warrior sings,
"The Lord's right hand doth valiant things."

I shall not die, but live to praise
The Lord, whose love prolongs my days,
The Lord, who sorely chasteneth,
But saves me from the snares of death.

Ope wide the gates of righteousness,
That I may enter in and bless
The Lord for His redeeming grace,
Adoring in His holy place.

This is the portal of the Lord:
Here enter they that keep His word.
"Hearer of prayer, I praise Thy Name,
By which my strong salvation came."

The stone the builders cast away
Stands the chief corner-stone to-day:
This work is from the Lord: to us
How great it seems, how marvellous!

This is the day the Lord hath made;
Rejoice we in it and be glad.
O Lord, Thy saving help, we pray,
O Lord, Thy blessing grant this day.—

'Be blessèd, ye that enter here,
That in Jehovah's Name appear:
We bless you from the Lord's abode,
We bless you from the house of God.

The Lord alone is God: His light
Shines through the darkness of our night.
Lead ye the festal victim, lead
And bind it to the altar's head.'—

Thou art my God; I praise Thy Name:
My God; I will exalt Thy fame.—
'Praise ye the Lord, for good is He;
His mercy lives eternally.'

PSALM CXIX. PART I.

How blest are they who flee from ill,
And keep the Lord's most holy will:
How blest who ne'er desert His way,
But with a perfect heart obey.

They venture on no lawless deed,
But follow where His precepts lead.
Thy Law was ratified of yore,
That we might keep it evermore.

O that some power my steps would guide
In thy commandments to abide:
Upon my face no shame will be,
When all Thy rules are dear to me.

My heart shall give Thee praise sincere,
Instructed in Thy righteous fear:
My guide shall be Thy sacred Word:
Forsake me not for ever, Lord.

Part II.

What skill shall keep the way of youth
In spotless innocence and truth?
Thy guiding power alone, O Lord;
The lessons of Thy holy Word.

I seek Thee with a mind sincere;
O keep me stedfast in Thy fear:
Thy words are hid my heart within,
So shall I never turn to sin.

O teach me, blessèd Lord, Thy ways:
The judgments of Thy mouth I praise
With upright lips, and prize them more
Than wealth in unexhausted store.

Thy precepts may I ponder still,
And have respect unto Thy will:
Such pure delight its rules impart,
Thy Word shall never quit my heart.

Part III.

Give life unto Thy servant, Lord;
So will I keep Thy holy Word:
Ope Thou mine eyes, that I may see
The wondrous things ordained by Thee.

A pilgrim on the earth I stray;
Thy laws, to light my path, display:
My soul is sick, and longeth sore
To see Thy judgments evermore.

The proud, the accurst ones, Thou dost chide,
Who from Thy statutes wander wide:
From shame and anguish set me free;
Thy counsels have been kept by me.

When slanderous chiefs misjudge my cause,
Thy servant thinks upon Thy laws:
My comfort and delight are they,
My counsellors in evil day.

PART IV.

My soul unto the dust is bowed;
  As Thou hast promised, quicken me:
Thou heardest, when my ways I showed;
  O Lord, Thy precepts let me see.

Teach me the way that I should go;
  So shall I muse upon Thy might:
My soul is weeping in its woe:
  O raise me, for Thine ancient plight.

Remove from me the path of lies,
  And show me graciously Thy Law;
I keep Thy rule before mine eyes,
  Nor from Thy truth my thoughts withdraw.

Thy testimonies guide me still;
  Put from me, Lord, reproach and shame;
My heart enlarged shall keep Thy will,
  And ever bless Thy saving Name.

PART V.

Teach me, O Lord, Thy righteous way,
  Thy counsels bid me follow still,
Instruct me ever to obey
  And keep Thy Law with perfect will.

Ne'er from Thy path my steps remove;
  My purest joys are found therein:
My heart incline, Thy truth to love
  And hate the losing gains of sin.

From vanity mine eyes withdraw,
  And in Thy ways revive me, Lord:
Thy servant holds Thy Name in awe;
  Fulfil to him Thy faithful word.

The scorn I fear dispel from me;
  Thy judgments all are good and true:
Thy righteousness I long to see;
  With Thy pure Law my heart renew.

PART VI.

O MAY Thy loving mercy find me, Lord,
  According to Thy gracious word.
Give me an answer to reviling foes;
  In Thy sure promise I repose.

Withdraw not from my lips a truthful voice,
  For in Thy judgments I rejoice:
So shall I do Thy will, Thy Name adore,
  For ever and for evermore.

In perfect liberty my feet shall move,
  Because I keep Thy Law of love:
Thy testimonies though to kings I speak,
  No shame shall kindle on my cheek.

In following Thy behests my heart is bright;
  They are my comfort and delight:
With lifted hands Thy loved commands I bless,
  And muse on all Thy righteousness.

PART VII.

O FULFIL unto Thy servant,
  Lord, Thy hope-inspiring word:
This was comfort in my sorrow,
  When Thy pleasant voice I heard.

Though the proud deride me greatly,
  From Thy Law I ne'er have fled:
Musing on Thine ancient judgments,
  Lord, my soul was comforted.

Wroth am I to view the wicked,
  Who Thy righteous Law forsake:
While I dwell on earth a pilgrim,
  All my song Thy statutes make.

In the night Thy Name recalling,
  I have kept Thy perfect will:
This Thy loving mercy granted,
  For I truly served Thee still.

Part VIII.

My portion is the living Lord;
I say that I will keep Thy Word:
I pray to Thee with heart sincere;
Thou with Thy promised favour hear.

I pondered well mine errors past,
And turned me to Thy paths at last:
I sped, and made no more delay,
Thy holy precepts to obey.

By snares of wicked men beset
Thy truth my soul doth ne'er forget:
At midnight hour I rise to bless
The judgments of Thy righteousness.

I league with friends who keep Thy Law
And hold Thy Name in sacred awe;
Earth with Thy plenteous love is stored:
O teach me all Thy statutes, Lord.

PART IX.

Well with Thy servant hast Thou dealt, O Lord,
  According to Thy word:
Sound intellect to me, with knowledge, give,
  For in Thy faith I live.

Before I was distrest I went astray,
  But now shall I obey.
Good art Thou, good Thou doest evermore;
  Teach me Thy righteous lore.

The proud speak lies of me; but in Thy fear
  I walk with heart sincere:
Their heart is fat as brawn; but in Thy will
  I find my pleasure still.

'Twas good for me to suffer, that I might
  Thy statutes learn aright:
Thousands of gold and silver glad me less
  Than Thy pure righteousness.

PART X.

Thy hands have made and fashioned me;
  O teach me, Lord, Thy will:
Who fear Thy Word with joy shall see
  That I have kept it still.

Just are Thy judgments: Thou dost smite
  In faithfulness, I know:
. Yet ah, redeem Thine ancient plight,
  And heal Thy servant's woe.

O send Thy grace that I may live;
  Thy Law is joy to me:
Defeat the slanderous foe, but give
  My soul to muse on Thee.

Returning friends shall take my part,
  Who know and fear Thy Name;
Sound in Thy statutes keep my heart,
  And free from sin and shame.

PART XI.

My soul is fainting for Thy Word of grace,
  And pants to see Thy saving face:
Mine eyes are failing for Thy truth, and say,
  Why doth our Comforter delay?

A bottle in the smoke resembling, yet
  Thy statutes ne'er do I forget.
How many are Thy servant's days, O Lord?
  When smites the foe Thy vengeful sword?

They have dug for me their pits, the lawless crew,
  Who none of Thy behests pursue.
Thy statutes all are faithful: wrongfully
  They persecute: but help Thou me.

Almost they had consumed me from the land;
  But I forsook not Thy command:
After the witness of Thy mouth to live,
  Good Lord, my quickened spirit give.

PART XII.

Everlasting art Thou, Lord;
Rests in heaven Thy settled Word:
Endless doth Thy truth endure;
Earth, Thy work, abides secure.

Ruled by Thee they stand to-day;
Thee must all, that is, obey.
Grief had slain me, but I saw
Strength and solace in Thy Law.

Quickened by Thy grace, my heart
From Thy faith shall ne'er depart:
I am Thine: my Saviour be,
For Thy precepts comfort me.

Plotting sinners lurk to kill,
But Thy truth I ponder still:
All perfection hath a close,
But Thy Law no limit knows.

PART XIII.

How dear, O Lord, Thy Law to me,
  My study and my ceaseless song!
  Thy statutes make me very strong,
Yea, wiser than mine enemy;
  For they are with me all day long.

More than my teachers do I know,
  For with Thy Word I commune still,
  And meditate Thy sacred will:
Thus living in Thy Truth I grow
  Profound above all ancient skill.

From every false and sinful way
  My cautious feet have I refrained,
  That I might keep Thy Word unstained:
Thy righteous judgments I obey;
  Such wisdom from Thy mouth I gained.

Thy words unto my taste how sweet,
  Sweeter than honey to my tongue!
  Wise counsels to Thy Law belong:
By these inspired, my willing feet
  Avoid the way of guile and wrong.

PART XIV.

UNTO my feet a lantern shines Thy Word,
    And to my paths a light;
An oath I sware, a binding oath, O Lord,
    To keep Thy rule of right.

O Lord, as Thou hast promised, so relieve
    My sorely laden heart:
The free-will offerings of my mouth receive,
    And Thy great truths impart.

My life is ever in my hand: but ne'er
    Do I forget Thy will;
And, though the wicked hunt me with a snare,
    I guard Thy precepts still.

Thy truths I make my deathless heritage,
    My heart's sincere delight;
Thy statutes to perform from age to age
    My purpose and my plight.

PART XV.

FICKLE hearts I ne'er approve,
But Thy stable Law I love,
Hoping in Thy Word of grace,
Lord, my shield and hiding-place.

Evil workers, hence away;
God's commandments I obey.
Guard my life; Thy truth I claim;
Bury not my hope in shame.

Stand and save me; so my heart
From Thy rule shall ne'er depart:
Thou o'erthrow'st the erring feet,
Baffled in their vain deceit.

Sin, as dross, Thine eyes repel;
Hence I love Thy statutes well:
All my flesh with trembling awe
Dreads the judgments of Thy Law.

PART XVI.

WITH truth and righteousness I deal:
Lord, to the foeman's proud control
Abandon not my trusting soul:
Be surety for Thy servant's weal.

I long for Thy salvation, Lord;
Mine eyes are pining for Thy grace:
Look on me with Thy loving face;
Unveil to me Thy glorious Word.

I am Thy servant: make me wise,
That I may know Thy rule of right:
'Tis time for Thee to prove Thy might,
O Lord, for men Thy Law despise.

Nor gold nor jewel is to me
So precious as Thy perfect will:
Hence do I guard Thy statutes still,
False ways abhorring utterly.

PART XVII.

THY laws my soul observes; so wondrous, Lord,
It sees their depth and height:
The simple understand Thy holy Word:
Its entrance giveth light.

I oped my mouth and panted: for my thirst
Desired Thy truth alone:
Look on me with the tender grace, which erst
Thy loving saints have known.

Rule with Thy Word my steps, and keep me free
    From all enslaving ill;
From persecuting foes deliver me,
    That I may do Thy will.

Upon Thy servant make Thy light to rise,
    And teach me all Thy lore;
Rivers of waters running from mine eyes
    Thy broken Law deplore.

PART XVIII.

JUST art Thou, Lord, Thy judgments true,
Thy counsels right, and faithful too:
My zeal consumes me: for I know
Thy Law forgotten by my foe.

Thy Word is very pure; that Word
Thy servant therefore loveth, Lord:
Small am I and despised, but yet
Thy precepts will I ne'er forget.

Thy righteousness no end shall see;
It lasteth to eternity:
Thy statutes evermore remain,
Thy Law is truth without a stain.

I pine with anguish and annoy,
But Thy commandments are my joy:
They never die: such doctrine give
My soul to understand, and live.

PART XIX.

WITH my whole heart call I to Thee:
    Hear me; I will keep Thy Word:
Yea, to Thee I call; O save me;
    I will keep Thy statutes, Lord.

Thee before the morn invoking
  All Thy truth I long to see;
Yea, before the nightly watches
  Wake mine eyes to muse on Thee.

Hear my voice, in love and pity;
  Guide me with Thy quickening light:
Nigh are those, who, bent on evil,
  Wander from Thy rule of right.

Nigh be Thou; Thy great commandments,
  Lord, are purest truth and grace:
Long I knew Thy laws were founded
  On a firm eternal base.

PART XX.

O LOOK upon my woes, and set me free;
  Thy laws I keep, O Lord;
Redress my righteous cause, and quicken me
  According to Thy word.

Far from the godless men is saving health,
  Who from Thy statutes rove:
As Thou art wont, revive me: great the wealth
  Of Thy redeeming love.

Though countless foes my perilled life pursue,
  To me Thy truths are dear:
It grieves me to behold the faithless crew,
  Who walk not in Thy fear.

Mark how I love Thy laws: O gracious Lord,
  My fainting soul restore:
Thy righteous judgments live, Thy Word of truth
  Endures for evermore.

Part XXI.

Though princes hunt my life with causeless hate,
　　I hold Thy Word in awe;
As warrior counting spoil with heart elate,
　　So, Lord, I greet Thy Law.

My shrinking heart abhors deceitful ways,
　　But Thy commands I love;
Seven times a day my songs of joyful praise
　　Thy rule of right approve.

Great peace have they who love Thy Law; they live
　　Exempt from all offence:
I hope for Thy salvation, Lord, and strive
　　To guard mine innocence.

My soul observes Thy testimonies still;
　　They are my true delight:
My heart is set to keep Thy perfect will:
　　My ways are in Thy sight.

Part XXII.

O hear me, Lord, instruct and save,
For the sweet hope Thy promise gave:
My lips shall be a fount of praise,
When Thou hast taught me all Thy ways.

Thy faithful Word my songs shall bless,
For Thy behests are righteousness:
O help me with Thy powerful hand;
I choose whate'er Thy rules command.

I long for Thy salvation, Lord,
And find my pleasure in Thy Word:
To sing Thy praise my soul revive,
And by Thy judgments let me live.

Like a lost sheep, I went astray,
And wandered from Thy pleasant way:
O seek Thy servant, save him yet;
Thy statutes do I ne'er forget.

PSALM CXX.

In trouble to the Lord I prayed;
  A gracious ear He deigned to lend:
'Save me from lying lips,' I said,
  'Lord, from the perjured tongue defend.'

What bring thy lips, thou lying foe?
  And what, false tongue, thy vile deceit?
Sharp arrows from a giant's bow,
  Fierce coals that burn with smouldering heat.

Alas, that I should still abide
  In Kedar's tents, with Meshech's clan,
That, where the foes of peace reside,
  I pine so long, a friendless man!

To peace alone I give my heart;
  But, when I speak a gentle word,
In scornful ire their warriors start,
  And brandish high the gleaming sword.

PSALM CXXI.

Mine eyes I lift unto the hills:
  Whence comes my promised aid?—
'From Him—the Lord, whose glory fills
  The heaven and earth He made.

May He sustain thy foot, and keep
  Around thee watch and ward:
He slumbereth not, He shall not sleep,
  Thy keeper, Israel's guard.

The Lord it is defends thy way,
   The Lord upon thy right,
That shades thee from the sun by day,
   And from the moon by night.

The Lord shall keep thee from all ill;
   Thy soul He watcheth o'er:
Thy going and thy coming still
   He keepeth evermore.'

PSALM CXXII.

'SEEK we Jehovah's house,' they said:
   O joyful invitation!
Stand we in Salem's gates, and tread
   The courts of our salvation.

O Salem, O thou city fair,
   And built in perfect union!
There march the tribes of Israel, there
   Give thanks in sweet communion;

Give thanks to Him, whose Name they bless,
   Of all their health the Giver:
There David's house in righteousness
   Sits throned to judge for ever.

Then pray we for our Salem's peace,
   And pray for all who love her:
Strong be her walls, her palaces
   With plenty running over:

For brethren's sake, and neighbours dear,
   The Lord our God befriend thee,
And in His holy place be near
   To prosper and defend thee.

PSALM CXXIII.

To Thee, great King, I lift my longing eyes,
    Whose throne is in the skies.
Lo, as the eyes of servants ever watch
    Their master's sign to catch;

As looks the maiden to her mistress still
    For tokens of her will;
So to the Lord our God we look, so trace
    The signals of His grace.

O gracious Lord, our sad and helpless state
    Do Thou compassionate:
For we have eaten of shame's bitter bread,
    And to the full are fed:

Yea, e'en to loathing take we for our food
    The insults coarse and rude
Of scornful wealth, and overweening wrongs
    From proud oppressive tongues.

PSALM CXXIV.

'Unless the Lord with us had wrought,'
    May Israel now rejoicing say,
'Unless the Lord for us had fought,
    When men against us rose to slay,

Our very lives they had devoured,
    So hotly blazed their angry mood;
Our fainting souls had sunk o'erpowered
    Within the proud and wasteful flood:

Yea, we had found a sudden grave
    Beneath the whelming torrent's sway;
But blest be He who sped to save,
    And from the spoiler snatched his prey.

Like birds we scaped the fowler's net;
  The meshes brake, and we are free:
Our help alone, O Lord, is set,
  Maker of heaven and earth, in Thee.'

PSALM CXXV.

WHO in the Lord securely lay
  Their firm-built faith, unmoved shall stand
  As Zion hill, which time's strong hand
Shall ne'er surrender to decay.

As mountains high on every side
  Engirdle fair Jerusalem,
  Such is their guardian Lord to them
Who stedfast in His love abide.

For though sometimes the Lord incline
  To smite the righteous, He will not
  Assign for their eternal lot
Beneath the scorner's rod to pine,

Lest they to foul iniquity
  Their yet untainted hands extend.
  To them, O Lord, Thy blessing send,
Whose upright hearts abhor a lie.

The sinner's latter end is hell,
  With all who turn to wickedness:
  But still our gracious Lord shall bless
With peace His chosen Israel.

PSALM CXXVI.

'TWAS dream-like, when the Lord's decree
Broke Zion's chain, and made us free:
But soon from each delighted tongue
Rose the gay laugh, the joyous song.

From realm to realm the tidings flew;
The wondrous sign the nations knew,
And 'Great,' they said, 'the gift bestowed
On these, the favoured of their God.'

'Yea, great the gift,' with heart and voice
We shout responding, and rejoice.
Bring home, O Lord, our captive bands,
As gushing streams to sunburnt lands.

Who sow in tears in joy shall reap:
The ploughman o'er his toil may weep,
But, when the teeming month is come,
He bears the sheaves exulting home.

PSALM CXXVII.

UNLESS the Lord the house erecteth,
    The builders' toil is fruitless pain,
Unless the Lord the town protecteth,
    The watchman waketh but in vain.

What boots to rise before the morrow,
    Nor ere the dead of night to rest?
Why eat the bread of useless sorrow,
    When His beloved in sleep are blest?

A gift from God are children yielded;
    The fruitful womb His blessing call;
As arrows by the warrior wielded
    Are sons within their father's hall.

Whose quiver such abundance graces,
    How happy he, how strong his state!
They meet his foes with dauntless faces,
    And parley with them in the gate.

PSALM CXXVIII.

Blest he who fears the Lord, and still
Walks in His ways and does His will:
Thy toiling hands shall yield thee food,
O happy soul, and rich in good.
Within thine house thy wife shall shine
As on thy walls the fruitful vine:
Thy sons, like olive-branches fair,
In youthful prime thy table share.

So shall the righteous man be blest,
The man who fears the Lord's behest.
The Lord from Zion's holy place
Assist thee with His constant grace,
And grant thee, through thy lifelong days,
On Salem's happiness to gaze,
To see thy children's seed increase,
And Israel's borders smile with peace.

PSALM CXXIX.

Oft from my childhood, Israel now may say,
    Afflictions were my lot,
Afflictions heavy from life's earliest day;
    Yet they subdued me not.

Long furrows on my back the ploughers scored,
    And grievous was my pain:
But to my rescue came the righteous Lord,
    And cut their bands in twain.

In shameful rout may Zion's haters flee,
    Defeated and o'erthrown;
Like grass upon the housetop may they be,
    That withereth ere 'tis grown.

It fills no mower's hand, no gleaners pluck
    Its ripeness for their hoard:
No passers cry, 'God prosper thee: good luck
    We wish thee from the Lord.'

PSALM CXXX.

Out of the depths to Thee I cry:
    Hear, Lord, my sad petition:
Be swift, O Lord, to heed; be nigh
    To save me from perdition.

If sin to strict account Thou call,
    Lord, who may stand before Thee?
But with Thee pardon dwells, that all
    May fear while they adore Thee.

I wait the Lord's redeeming grace;
    My soul for Him is yearning
More eagerly than watchmen trace
    The daylight's sweet returning.

O Israel, make the Lord thy stay;
    With Him is rich salvation:
His love will put thy sins away,
    And bless His chosen nation.

PSALM CXXXI.

Lord, I am not lofty-minded,
    No proud looks have I:
Never, with presumption blinded,
    Soar my thoughts too high.

I have tasked my soul discreetly
    Meek and still to be,
Like a weanling cradled sweetly
    On its mother's knee.

Israel, be thy hope abiding
Stedfast in the Lord,
Now and evermore confiding
In His changeless Word.

PSALM CXXXII.

REMEMBER David, Lord, and all his pain,
  How to the Lord he sware a solemn plight,
  And vowed a vow to Jacob's worshipped Might:
'Nor home, nor bed, nor sleep be mine again,

Mine eyelids rest not, till the Lord shall own
  A shrine, and Israel's Strength a meet abode.'—
  At Ephrath heard we of the ark of God;
At length we found it in the forest-town.

Now to His tabernacle let us come,
  Before His footstool let us humbly bow:
  'Arise, O Lord, into Thy dwelling now;
Thou, with Thy ark of strength, here make Thy home.

In holy raiment stand Thy priestly train;
  With shouting glee Thy worshippers rejoice:
  O hear Thy servant David's suppliant voice,
Nor let Thine own Anointed plead in vain.'

A faithful oath the Lord to David sware,
  Nor from His plighted word will ever flee:
  'Upon thy throne thy body's fruit shall be;
Yea, if thy seed, from heir to distant heir,

Shall keep My covenant with upright heart,
  Nor scorn the lessons of My sacred lore,
  From them and from their children nevermore
The royal throne of David shall depart.

The hill of Zion to the Lord is dear,
  The chosen temple of His heavenly grace;
  This is from age to age My resting-place;
Here will I dwell; for My desire is here.

Her store with rich abundance I will bless;
  With bread her needy shall be satisfied,
  Her priests be clothed with power, and far and wide
Her courts shall ring with saintly mirthfulness.

Here will I make the horn of David grow:
  A lamp for Mine Anointed I will light,
  And clothe his foes with shame: but ever bright
The crown shall flourish on his stately brow.'

PSALM CXXXIII.

BEHOLD, how good it is, how sweet,
In mutual love when brethren meet!
'Tis like the precious ointment shed
On Aaron's consecrated head,

That o'er his beard went trickling down
Even to the border of his gown:
Like Hermon's dew, which eve distils
To fall on holy Zion's hills:

For there the glorious Lord of heaven
Blessing and happy life has given,
Blessing in unexhausted store,
And happy life for evermore.

PSALM CXXXIV.

BLESS ye the Lord; His solemn praise record,
    Ye servants of the Lord,
Ye that within His sacred temple stand,
    A nightly-watching band,

Lift up your hands within His holy place,
    And veil the prostrate face,
And bless ye there the Lord, adore and bless
    The Lord your righteousness.

'May He who made the earth and heavenly height,
    Lord of all power and might,
From Zion's mount His endless blessings shed
    Upon thy favoured head.'

PSALM CXXXV. Part I.

Praise ye the Lord, His Name adored
Extol, ye servants of the Lord;
Who, stationed in the Lord's abode,
Frequent the temple-courts of God.
Praise ye the gracious Lord, proclaim
The splendour of His lovely Name.

The Lord in Jacob chose to dwell,
His shrine He placed in Israel.
I know the Lord is great; our Lord
Above all gods to be adored:
Whate'er He willed in secret thought
His wondrous power in heaven has wrought,

In earth and all unfathomed caves,
Where ocean hides its wealth of waves.
From limitary coasts of earth
He brings the vaporous clouds to birth;
His lightnings glare through rainy skies;
The storm-blast from His chamber flies.

PART II.

Egypt's first-born seed He slew,
Seed of men and cattle too:
Yea, proud Egypt, all thy land
Saw His wonder-working hand
Pharaoh's head with vengeance smite,
Scatter Pharaoh's men of might.

Many a nation sank o'erthrown;
Mighty princes He struck down,
Sihon, Amoritish lord,
Og, the chief of Bashan's horde:
Canaan's hosts before Him fell,
And His people Israel

Held of Him from age to age
All their lands in heritage.
Lord, eternal is Thy Name,
Sire to son reports Thy fame:
For the Lord with gentlest grace
Judgeth His repentant race.

Gods of silver and of gold,
Blocks which human fingers mould,
Heathens worship foolishly:
Eyes they have, but cannot see;
Speechless lips, unhearing ears,
Mouths devoid of breath are theirs:

Dull as these are they that frame,
And who trust them are the same.
Bless the Lord, all ye who count
Your descent from Israel's fount:
Bless the Lord, all ye that claim
Priestly worth from Aaron's name:

Bless the Lord, O Levi's line,
Sacred watchers of His shrine:
Bless the Lord with holy fear,
Ye that in His courts appear.
Blessèd be the Lord, whose might
Salem guards from Zion's height. Hallelujah!

PSALM CXXXVI.

PRAISE the Lord, for good is He;
   Praise Him to the ringing chords,
Praise Him with melodious glee,
   God of gods and Lord of lords:
For His mercy full and free
Lasteth to eternity.

Rich in wisdom, rich in love,
   Are the wonders of His hand;
Thus He reared the heaven above,
   Thus He spread the sea-girt land:
For His mercy full and free
Lasteth to eternity.

O'er the heavenly vault on high
   Lamps He hung in order bright;
Sun to rule the daily sky,
   Moon and stars to reign by night:
For His mercy full and free
Lasteth to eternity.

Egypt's first-born seed He slew:
   Israel's thousands, safe from harm,
Out of bondage He withdrew
   With strong hand and outstretcht arm:
For His mercy full and free
Lasteth to eternity.

He the Red-sea billows clave:
   Israel fled the hostile coast:
In the wild rebounding wave
   Pharaoh sank with all his host:
For His mercy full and free
Lasteth to eternity.

Through the waste His own He led,
   Led the seed He loved so well;
Mighty kings before Him fled,
   Mighty kings before Him fell:
For His mercy full and free
Lasteth to eternity.

Sihon, royal Amorite,
   Og of Bashan—vain their rage:
He to strong subduing might
   Gave their realms in heritage:
For His mercy full and free
Lasteth to eternity.

He the conquered lands in fee
   To His servant Israel gave:
In our troubles swift was He
   From the foeman's power to save:
For His mercy full and free
Lasteth to eternity.

His the bounty that conveys
   To all flesh its daily food:
To the God of heaven give praise,
   Praise and thanks: for He is good,
And His mercy full and free
Lasteth to eternity.

PSALM CXXXVII.

We sat and wept by Babel's stream,
For Zion was our mournful theme:
And there, on many a willow bough,
We hung our harps, all silent now.

They came, whose captive yoke we bear,
They came and saw us weeping there:
A mirthful song they bade us raise:
'Come, sing us one of Zion's lays.'

How shall I chant to stranger's ear
A song the Lord was pleased to hear?
If I forget thee, Zion hill,
May my right hand forget her skill;

My tongue let cleaving palsy chain
When from my heart thy memories wane,
When thou, Jerusalem, shalt be
Than any joy less dear to me.

O Lord, requite on Edom's name
Thy Salem's day of grief and shame;
When, 'Rase her,' envious Esau cried,
'Rase to the ground her towering pride.'

Daughter of Babel, on thy walls
The stroke of vengeful ruin falls:
And blest the man whose arms redress
Our woes on thee, proud conqueress:

Yea, blest the warrior prince shall be,
Who turns thy cruelties on thee,
Who grasps thy helpless little ones,
And dashes them against the stones.

PSALM CXXXVIII.

With my whole heart I will praise Thee;
  I will hymn the Name Divine,
In the presence of the mighty
  Bowing down before Thy shrine.

For Thy truth and for Thy mercy
  Will I bless Thy Name, O Lord,
Name most highest, yet more highly
  Thou hast magnified Thy Word.

When my suppliant prayer has sought Thee,
  Still Thy promised grace was nigh,
To my faithful heart conveying
  Strength and hope and courage high.

All the kings of earth shall praise Thee,
  When Thy solemn voice they hear,
Of Thy goodness, of Thy glory,
  They shall sing with humble fear.

For the Lord, so high exalted,
  On the lowly looks with love,
But He notes the haughty spirit
  With displeasure from above.

Me in trouble Thou revivest:
  And, when foes against me rave,
Thou Thy strong right-hand extendest,
  Strong, and merciful to save.

Mine shall be all earthly blessings,
  If the Lord vouchsafe His aid:
Lord, Thy love is never-ending;
  Bless the work Thy hands have made. .

PSALM CXXXIX.

O Lord, Thou searchest all my ways,
　And well Thou knowest me:
My sitting down, my rising up,
　They are espied by Thee.

Thou understandest from afar
　The musings of my heart;
Around my daily path, around
　My nightly bed Thou art.

Ere any sound is on my tongue,
　Thou hear'st the unuttered word;
Thou girdest me behind, before;
　Thy hand is on me, Lord.

O knowledge wonderful and high,
　Too excellent for me!
Thy Spirit how shall I escape,
　Or from Thy presence flee?

If to the farthest heaven I soar,
　The heaven is Thine abode:
If in the grave I make my bed,
　Lo, Thou art there, O God.

If on the wings of morn I fly,
　And dwell beyond the sea,
E'en there Thy hand shall lead me still,
　Thy right-hand holdeth me:

And if I say, 'the falling shade
　Will surely veil my way,'
The shadows flee before my face,
　And night is changed to day.

To Thee the darkness is not dark,
  Nor day more clear than night:
Yea, both alike to Thee they shine,
  The darkness and the light.

Thou art the founder of my life,
  My reins belong to Thee:
Within my mother's womb of yore
  Thy wisdom fashioned me.

My frame, so dread, so wonderful,
  Its Maker's praise shall tell:
How marvellous are all Thy works
  My soul it knoweth well.

My substance lay not hid from Thee:
  Thou saw'st my secret birth,
When I was woven cunningly
  Beneath the silent earth.

Thine eyes beheld my outlined form,
  My days were written down
Within Thy Book; to Thee were all,
  Before their coming, known.

How precious are my thoughts of Thee,
  How passing great their sum,
More than the sand, O God! at morn
  I wake, and still they come.

Destroy the wicked foes, O God;
  The men of blood refrain,
Who speak of Thee with lying lips,
  And take Thy Name in vain.

Hate I not them that hate Thee, Lord?
  Am I not grieved with those
That menace Thee? with hatred deep
  I count them as my foes.

Search me, O God, and prove my heart
  E'en to its inmost ground:
Try me, and know my thoughts, if aught
  Of evil there be found:

O never let my careless feet
  In paths of sorrow stray,
But lead me faithfully to keep
  The everlasting way.

PSALM CXL.

REDEEM me from the lawless might
  Of wicked men, O Lord;
Who gather daily for the fight,
  An evil-minded horde:
They whet their teeth, as serpents fell;
Their lips with adder's poison swell.

Lord, save me from the foeman's wrath:
  Defeat the sons of strife,
Who place their ambush in my path,
  To snare my perilled life:
Their cord is hid and spread their net;
Their traps for me the proud have set.

Unto the Lord I cried at length;
  'Thou art my God alone:
Lord, hear my cry:' my saving strength
  From God the Lord is shown:
My head Thou coverest in the day
When hosts are rushing to the fray.

Lord, pamper not their haughty mood,
  Nor grant their wicked will,
Who prowl around, a godless brood,
  Intent on mischief still:
The sorrows which their lips have bred
Make Thou the covering of their head:

Let burning coals upon them fall:
  With Thine avenging ire
Full swiftly strike, and hurl them all
  Within the gulph of fire:
Beneath the whelming torrent's roar
They soon shall sink, to rise no more.

The slanderous tongue shall fail, the foe
  Shall perish in his spite:
The Lord upholds the weak, I know,
  And guards the poor man's right:
Thy praise the ransomed just shall tell;
Before Thy face the meek shall dwell.

PSALM CXLI.

To Thee I call: O Lord, be swift
  To hear my earnest cries;
Before Thy presence let my prayer
  As fragrant incense rise,
And be the lifting of my hands
  An evening sacrifice.

Lord, set a watch before my mouth,
  My guarded lips make fast:
Turn not my heart to men, whose thoughts
  On wickedness are cast:
Ne'er let me do their sinful deeds,
  Nor of their dainties taste.

The just shall smite in love: his oil
  Upon my head I lay
As healing balm:—against the sin
  Of men unjust I pray:
Their princes, flung on rocks, shall hear
  My words, how sweet are they.

Our bones, as cut and cloven logs,
  Beside the pit are strown:
But unto Thee we look for health,
  To Thee we make our moan:
Shed not the life which hangs on Thee,
  O Lord my Lord, alone.

From snares by crafty foes contrived
  Do Thou deliver me,
And from the wicked scorner's net:
  Let sinners tangled be
In their own toils, while I pass on
  From pain and peril free.

PSALM CXLII.

Unto the Lord I make my moan,
  My prayers unto the Lord arise;
  To Him I pour my frequent sighs
And tell my griefs to Him alone.

For when my soul is faint and low,
  Thy loving eyes discern my way,
  Though secret snares the godless lay
Along the path wherein I go.

I look unto the right, and there
  Behold no sympathizing eye,
  No shelter, whither I may fly,
No helper, for my soul to care.

Before Thy face, O Lord, I stand,
  And say: 'My only trust Thou art,
  The stay and solace of my heart,
My portion in the living land.

O hearken to my prayer: I pine
  And die away with endless woes;
  O quell my persecuting foes,
For stronger is their arm than mine.

My weary soul from thrall release,
  That I may bless Thy Name in song:
  Around me shall the righteous throng,
When Thou shalt give me joy and peace.'

PSALM CXLIII.

HEAR Thou my prayer, O Lord,
  And listen to my cry:
O think upon Thy faithful word,
  And graciously reply.

O not in judgment rise
  Thy servant's life to scan;
For righteous in Thy spotless eyes
  Is found no living man.

My cruel-minded foes
  Crush to the earth my head:
In darkness dwells my life, as those
  Whose home is with the dead:

My fainting heart is cold
  Even to its inmost core:
I muse upon the days of old,
  Thy ways and works of yóre;

I stretch my longing hands
  Toward Thy holy place,
With soul athirst, like weary lands,
  For Thy refreshing grace.

Haste Thee, O Lord, I pray,
  My failing heart to save:
Hide not Thy face: I droop as they
  That sink into the grave.

Thy mercy's dawning light
  My faith desires to see:
O let me walk before Thy sight:
  I lift my soul to Thee.

O guard me from the foe
  Within Thy strong abode:
Teach me, O Lord, Thy will to do;
  Thou art mine only God.

Let Thy good Spirit lead
  My feet in upright ways:
And for Thy Name's sake, Lord, my head
  From whelming troubles raise.

Perish the men of strife;
  On me let mercy shine:
Yea, perish all who seek my life;
  For I am wholly Thine.

PSALM CXLIV.

Praised be the Lord, my rock of might,
Who trains my fingers for the fight,
My Saviour kind, my fort, my tower,
My trusty shield in peril's hour,
Whose guiding hand confirms my sway,
And makes my people to obey.

Lord, what is man, that in Thy mind
His works and ways remembrance find?
Or what the mortal's son, to share
Thy tender love, Thy guardian care?
His scanty days, as shadows, flee,
And man is nought but vanity.

O Lord, Thy cloudy pillars bend,
And in Thy majesty descend:
Descend with pealing thunder-stroke,
And touch the mountains, till they smoke;
Disturb them with Thy flashing ire,
And rend them with Thy shafts of fire.

Thine arm outstretching from above,
Redeem me with Thy watchful love:
O pluck me from the whelming wave,
And from the stranger's malice save,
Whose mouth is full of flatteries,
And their right-hand a hand of lies.

A new-made song to God we raise;
The chorded harp shall swell His praise:
Spared from the peril of the sword,
Let prince and people bless the Lord,
The God of hosts, by whom alone
Our fields are fought, our victories won.

Lord, save us from the stranger's wrong,
The glozing lip, the perjured tongue:
As youthful saplings, rear our sons;
Fair as the temple's polished stones,
So fair, so strong, our daughters be,
And taught to love and worship Thee.

O fill our garners o'er and o'er
With corn and wine, a plenteous store;
Let thousand and ten thousand lambs
Leap in the field beside their dams:
Preserve in strength the labouring steer,
And bless our toil from year to year.

No widow's shriek, no orphan's moan,
No captive's deep despairing groan
Afflict our streets! O happy case!
O blessed and thrice-blessed race,
Whose trust is in their Saviour's Word,
Whose God is none but Zion's Lord!

PSALM CXLV.

EVER, O my God and King,
   I will exalt Thy fame,
Evermore Thy praises sing,
   And celebrate Thy Name.
Thee my voice shall magnify,
   My songs of daily worship bless;
Glorious is the Lord and high,
   His power is measureless.

Race to race shall still recite,
   And land proclaim to land
All Thy fearful acts of might,
   The wonders of Thy hand.

I will praise Thy majesty,
  The beauty of Thy beaming face;
Ne'er forgotten let them be,
  Thy righteousness and grace.

Slow to anger, rich in love,
  The Lord is ever good:
O'er His creatures from above
  His tender mercies brood.
All Thy creatures bless Thee, Lord;
  All godly men Thy power proclaim;
All Thy mighty deeds record,
  And glorify Thy Name:

Through the world the just make known
  Thy splendour and Thy might:
Everlasting is Thy crown,
  Thy kingdom infinite.
Feeble backs and sinking knees
  The Lord upholds with gentle hand;
He the o'erthrown with pity sees,
  And bids them rise and stand.

Every living eye to Thee
  Looks up for timely food;
And Thy hand is opened free
  To fill them all with good.
Just in all His ways the Lord,
  And in His doings ever kind,
Loves the saints who trust His word
  And pray with upright mind.

Who with humble fear draw nigh,
  He meets them with His grace,
Saves the loving when they cry,
  But smites the godless race.

Ever shall my mouth adore
  The Lord, and magnify His fame;
All my flesh for evermore
  Shall bless His holy Name.

PSALM CXLVI.

Praise the Lord, His people: raise,
O my soul, the note of praise:
I will praise the Lord till death,
Spend in praise my latest breath.

Not in princes put your trust,
Not in man, the child of dust:
Unavailing he to save
Hastens to the silent grave,

And in dark oblivion laid
All his projects with him fade.
Blest, whom Jacob's God defends,
On the Lord whose hope depends;

For the heavens, the earth, the sea,
And all things that in them be,
God created with His hand,
God whose laws unshaken stand.

He will right the injured head,
Feed the hungry soul with bread:
He unties the captive's chain,
Gives the blind his sight again:

He the widow's cause protects,
Nor the orphan's suit rejects;
Lifts the trampled from the dust,
Guards the stranger, loves the just.

Smiting sinners with His rod
Ever reigneth Zion's God,
Lord of all: with glad acclaim
Let us praise His hallowed Name.

PSALM CXLVII.

PRAISE the Lord: for it is wise
   Unto God a psalm to sing:
Praise is pleasant exercise,
   Giving thanks a goodly thing.

He doth build Jerusalem,
   Judah's outcasts gathering in:
Broken hearts—He healeth them,
   Binding up the wounds of sin.

He can tell the starry train,
   Every shining name recite:
Great in power the Lord doth reign,
   And in wisdom infinite.

He is nigh the meek to raise,
   Casting scorners to the ground;
Sing ye to our God with praise,
   Sing with harp's melodious sound.

With His clouds the sky He fills;
   On the earth His rain He pours,
Till the high and bárren hills
   Teem with grass and bloom with flowers.

Food to beast His hands allot,
   Ravens' crying nests they feed:
Strength of horse He prizes not,
   Little recks of human speed:

Fearing souls—He values them,
  Souls that for His mercy wait;
Praise the Lord, Jerusalem,
  Zion, praise Him: God is great.

He makes strong thy barrèd gates,
  Blessing showers upon thy seed;
In thy border peace creates,
  Fills thee full with wheaten bread.

Earth His strong command receives;
  Flies His word from coast to coast;
Snow, like flakes of wool, He gives,
  And, like ashes, scatters frost.

Morsel-like His ice is felt;
  Who can bear the chilling throe?
At His voice the glaciers melt:
  By His wind the waters flow.

All His sacred will He showed
  To the seed He loves so well,
Laws on Jacob He bestowed,
  Judgments gave to Israel.

For none other earthly race
  Love like this our God hath stored;
None, like us, have known His grace:
  Hallelujah! praise the Lord!

PSALM CXLVIII.

Praise the Lord from heaven on high:
Praise Him in the farthest sky;
Praise Him, all His angels bright,
Praise Him, all His hosts of light.

Praise Him, sun and moon and star,
Shining in the heavens afar:
Praise Him, height of height: His Name,
Water-floods aloft, proclaim.

Let them praise Him: for He spoke,
And to life His creatures woke,
Stablished evermore to be
Faithful to the Lord's decree.

Praise the Lord from earth below,
Fire and hail and rain and snow,
Storms that on His mandate sweep,
Whales, and every seething deep:

Mountains, and all hilly glades,
Fruit-trees, and vast cedarn shades,
Wild beast, and the gentler herds,
Creeping things, and feathered birds:

Kings of earth, and judges all,
Prince and people, great and small,
Stalwart youth, and maiden fair,
Babes, and men of hoary hair.

Let them praise Him: He the Lord,
Only Name to be adored,
Crowns with life and light and love
Earth beneath and heaven above.

He to all His saints is nigh,
Lifts His people's horn on high,
Guards His chosen Israel's fame:—
Praise, O praise His hallowed Name.

PSALM CXLIX.

O PRAISE ye the Lord,
  a new song prepare,
His praise with the saints
  assembled to sing:
Let Israel rejoicing
  his Maker declare,
And children of Zion
  be glad in their King.

His Name let them praise
  with pipe and with dance,
With timbrel and harp
  His glory confess:
The Lord taketh pleasure
  His saints to advance,
And with His salvation
  the righteous to bless.

Aloud let the meek
  exult in their joy,
Aloud on their bed
  give thanks to the Lord;
Be God's lofty praises
  their mouth's sweet employ,
And in their hand gleaming
  a two-edgèd sword;

The realms to chastise,
  the heathen to smite,
Their kings and their chiefs
  with fetters to load,

To execute on them
   the doom that is writ:—
His saints have such honour.
   O praise ye our God.

PSALM CL.

O PRAISE ye the Lord:
   praise Him in His shrine,
Praise Him in His strength
   of greatness divine:
Praise Him for His wonders,
   praise Him for His might,
So matchless in grandeur,
   in glory so bright.

Praise Him with the trump
   and clarion's swell,
His praise on the harp
   and psaltery tell;
Praise Him with the timbrel,
   the dance-loving flute,
Praise Him to the tabor
   and sweet-stringèd lute.

With cymbal's loud clash
   exalt ye His fame,
Let cymbals of mirth
   His splendour proclaim:
By all breathing creatures
   His Name be adored,
His glory be sounded:—
   O praise ye the Lord.

DOXOLOGIES.

As Psalm I.

Give glory to the Three in One,
  Ye saints and heavenly host,
To God the Father, God the Son,
  And God the Holy Ghost.

As Psalm IV.

1 Be God, the Father, Son,
    And Holy Ghost, adored,
The everlasting Three in One,
    The universal Lord.

2 We, with the angel host,
    Praise, honour, and adore
The Father, Son, and Holy Ghost,
    One God for evermore.

As Psalm V.

1 Praise Father, Son, and Holy Ghost,
    The God who was of yore,
Who is to-day, and shall abide
    One God for evermore.

2 To Father, Son, and Holy Ghost,
    One God whom we adore,
Be glory, as it was, and is,
    And shall be evermore.

As Psalm VI.

One God above, the Father, Son,
   And Holy Spirit, we revere,
The everlasting Three in One,
   Creator, Saviour, Comforter.

As Psalm VIII.

1 Praise God from whom all blessings flow,
   Praise Him, ye creatures here below,
   Praise Him above, angelic host,
   Praise Father, Son, and Holy Ghost.

2 The Father, Son, and Spirit bless,
   And Him the very God confess,
   Who was, and is, and is to be,
   The Godhead One, the Persons Three.

3 Praise we the Lord with choral hymn,
   To whom the harping Seraphim
   Their songs of endless joy repeat,
   The Father, Son, and Paraclete.

As Psalm IX.

Father, all-creating Love,
   Son, the Saviour ever blest,
Holy Spirit, heavenly Dove,
   Messenger of peace and rest,
Thee our grateful songs adore,
God, our God, for evermore.

DOXOLOGIES.

As Psalm XI.

Before His everlasting throne
Praise God the Father, God the Son,
And God the Spirit, Three in One

As Psalm XXIV.

To God the Father let us sing,
  The Author of creation;
To God the Son, our Lord and King,
  Who died for our salvation:
May God the Holy Spirit move
All hearts to bless, and praise, and love
  The One true God eternal.

As Psalm XXV.

1 God the Father, God the Son,
    God the Holy Ghost we bless;
  Persons Three in Godhead One
    We with faithful hearts confess.

2 God the Father let us bless,
    God the Son with praise adore.
  God the Holy Ghost confess
    One with these for evermore.

As Psalm XXVIII.

1 Glory be to God above,
    Fountain of eternal love;
  To the Father and the Son,
    And the Spirit, Three in One.

2 Father, guard us from above,
   Saviour, bless us with Thy love,
   Spirit, on our spirits shine,
   Make and keep us ever Thine.

As Psalm XXXIII.

All ye creatures, come, and clap your hands,
  Of your God with shouts of triumph boast;
Let His Name be known in utmost lands
  As the Father, Son, and Holy Ghost,
Who in Godhead One, in Persons Three,
Was, and is, and evermore shall be.

As Psalm XXXVI.

1 Sing everlasting praises to the Lord;
     By earthly creatures and the heavenly host
     Be God, the Father, Son, and Holy Ghost,
   Creator, Saviour, Comforter, adored.

2 O Father, evermore our Father be:
     O Son, the Saviour, save and bless us still:
     O guiding Spirit, work in us to will
   And do the things well pleasing unto Thee.

As Psalm XXXVII.

1 Glory be to God the Father,
     Glory be to God the Son,
   Glory be to God the Spirit,
     Co-eternal Three in One.

2 Father, our divine Creator,
     Son, the Saviour of our race,
   Spirit, our Regenerator,
     Guard and help us with Thy grace.

3 God, the Father of creation,
   Son, the Saviour of mankind,
Spirit of illumination,
   Make us Thine in heart and mind.

As PSALM XXXIX.

Ye choristers of earth,
   Ye quires of heaven, seraphic host,
Praise God with sacred mirth,
   The Father, Son, and Holy Ghost,
Who was, and is, and is to be
One God through all eternity.

As PSALM XL.

Be Father, Son, and Spirit blest,
   And very God confess'd,
Who was, and is, and is to be
   One God in Persons Three.

As PSALM XLI.

O Father, all-creating Love,
   O saving Son,
O quickening Spirit, holy Dove :—
   O Godhead One
In Persons Three, with light divine
Inspire our souls, and make them Thine.

As PSALM XLIV.

One God unseen, the Father, Son,
   And Holy Spirit, we revere,
   Creator, Saviour, Comforter,
The Persons Three, the Godhead One.

2 Ye saints of earth and heavenly host,
   With holy worship bend the knee
   Before the blessed Trinity:
 Praise Father, Son, and Holy Ghost.

As Psalm XLVII.

All ye creatures, come, and clap your hands,
  Of our God with shouts of gladness boast:
Let His Name be known in utmost lands,
  God the Father, Son, and Holy Ghost.

As Psalm L.

The Father's providence, the Son's salvation,
  The Spirit's light, with glad thanksgivings bless;
  The Trinity in Unity confess
With honour, praise, and humble adoration.

As Psalm LVI.

O Father, all-creating Love,
  O Son, the Saviour ever blest,
O Spirit, pure and holy Dove,
  Who bringest strength and joy and rest,
O Triune God, upon us shine,
And make and keep us wholly Thine.

As Psalm LVIII.

Sing praises to our God, the Father, Son,
  And Spirit, Three in One, who was of old,
    Who is, and will abide
      Through ages without end.

DOXOLOGIES.

As PSALM LXII.

The Father, whose creative word
  Called from the dust this wondrous frame,
  The Son, by whom salvation came,
The Spirit, soul-renewing Lord,
  Three Persons and One God, proclaim.

As PSALM LXIX. PART I.

O God, in whom alone we live and move,
  O Father blest,
O Son, O Spirit, fill us with Thy love,
  And give us rest.

As PSALM LXXII. PART II.

Praise with songs of exultation,
Bless with endless adoration,
  O ye saints, and angel host,
God the Maker and Provider,
God the Saviour, God the Guider,
  Father, Son, and Holy Ghost.

As PSALM LXXXV.

To Him who made us and controls,
  To Him who wrought salvation,
To Him who strengthens, guides, consoles,
  Sing praise and adoration,
The choral chant of morning stars
  When worlds were first created,
The song which God's redeemed will sing
  O'er worlds annihilated.

As Psalm LXXXVIII.

Praise God, the Lord of all creation,
   Ye saints of earth and heavenly host;
   The Father, Son, and Holy Ghost
Extol with songs of adoration.

As Psalm LXXXIX. Part II.

Ye saints of earth, and heavenly host,
The Father, Son, and Holy Ghost
   With endless praise adore,
Creator, Saviour, Guide of man,
One God, who reigned ere time began,
   And reigns for evermore.

As Psalm XCIII.

Ye saints of God, the Father bless,
The Son with thankful joy confess,
   The Holy Ghost adore;
Creator, Saviour, Guide of man,
One God, who was ere time began,
   Who is, and shall abide for evermore.

As Psalm XCVIII.

Ye saints, with heaven's adoring host,
Aloud proclaim from coast to coast
One God, the Father, Son, and Holy Ghost.

As Psalm CI.

With the great angelic host
   Our faithful hearts adore
Father, Son and Holy Ghost,
   One God for evermore.

Father, guard us with Thy love;
  Son, let us Thy salvation claim;
Holy Ghost, our spirits move
  To glorify Thy Name.

As Psalm CIV.

Praise to the Father let us sing,
  And blessing to the Son,
And worship to the Spirit bring,
  Co-equal Three in One,
Who was, and is, and is to be
The only God eternally.

As Psalm CXVIII.

All adoration be to Him,
Whom choirs of veilèd seraphim
Around the throne of glory sing,
The eternal Lord, the mighty King,
Who was, and is, and is to be
One God in equal Persons Three.

As Psalm CXXVII.

O Father, our divine Creator,
  O Son, the Saviour of our race,
O Spirit, our Regenerator,
  Assist and bless us with Thy grace.

As Psalm CXXIX.

Sing to the Lord, and loud your voices raise
  To His sublime abode;
The Father, Son, and Holy Spirit praise,
  Three Persons, and One God.

As Psalm CXLI.

Let all the dedicated host,
  Beloved of God on high,
With endless adoration bless
  And voice of melody
The Father, Son, and Holy Ghost,
  One God eternally.

As Psalm CXLIX.

Ye angels that shine
  around His bright throne,
Ye creatures on earth,
  your Maker adore:
O praise ye the Father,
  and bless ye the Son,
And worship the Spirit,
  One God evermore.

As Psalm CL.

O praise ye the Lord:
  the Father and Son
And Spirit exalt,
  Divine Three in One:
Whose wonderful essence
  existed of yore,
And is and continues
  the same evermore.

INDEX I.

BOOK I.

PSALM I. The blessedness of the righteous and ruin of the wicked.

II. The great ones of the earth rebel in vain against the Lord and His Messiah. (2 Sam. vii.)

III. Surrounded by many foes, David puts his *trust* in the Lord, whose protection he had already experienced, and *prays* to Him. (2 Sam. xv. 16.)

IV. David *prays* at evening, and *trusts* to God for help against his foes, with whom he reasons upon their folly. (2 Sam. xv.)

V. David earnestly *prays* in the morning for protection against treacherous and godless foes to that God who abhors sinners and defends all who *trust* in Him. (2 Sam. xx.)

VI. Faint in body and soul, and surrounded with enemies, David flees to God for help, and gains the *assurance* of support. (2 Sam. xx.)

VII. David *prays* for deliverance from cruel enemies; pleads his own innocence; appeals to God as the upright judge, to save the righteous and overthrow the guilty; assured of redress, he concludes with *thanksgiving*. (1 Sam. xxiv.)

VIII. The greatness of God in the greatness of man. (1 Sam. xxv.)

IX. God is *praised* for helping His people and humbling their foes: and then addressed in *prayer*, to help them still against other foes, and to humble the heathen. (2 Sam. xxi.)

X. David complains that the Lord's people are surrendered to godless enemies: he *prays* for redress, and in faith sees God's justice executed on sinners, and the just reinstated. (2 Sam. xxi.)

XI. In time of persecution, being advised to fly, David declares his full *confidence* in God's power, justice and providence. (2 Sam. xxi.)

XII. *Praying* against a corrupt world, David receives a favourable answer from the Lord, and declares his *trust* therein. (2 Sam. xxiii.)

XIII. Deeply distressed, and seemingly forgotten by the Lord, David *prays*, and places all his *trust* in God's goodness. (1 Sam. xxvii.)

XIV. Corruption and wickedness of the world, which God will punish, while He protects His saints: *hope* of a joyful salvation for Israel. (2 Sam.)

XV. Character of the man who is received by the Lord. (2 Sam. v.)

XVI. David declares his devotion to God, his affection for God's people, his abhorrence of idolatry; his blessedness as a servant of God: his *assurance* of preservation by God, even from the power of the grave. See the application to the resurrection of Christ, Acts ii. 24 &c. xiii. 35 &c. (1 Sam. xxx.)

XVII. David appeals to God, on the ground of his uprightness, for protection from foes, whose malice he describes: and concludes with *assured hope* of God's favour. (1 Sam. xxiv.)

XVIII. David *praises* God, whose power in delivering him he magnifies with fine imagery; ascribes God's favour to his own integrity; gives God the glory of his own victories; and rejoices in the *assurance* of His help. (2 Sam. xxii.)

XIX. The *praise* of God's glory in creation leads to the praise of His glory as giving the moral law, and this to a *prayer* for pardon, guidance, and preservation. (1 Sam. xxv.)

XX. The people declare their *hope* that the Lord will give victory to their king, and their confidence that God will not forsake His Anointed, but hear their *prayer* and his. (2 Sam. x.)

XXI. The people exult in the blessing conferred by the Lord upon their king: they *trust* that through God he will destroy all enemies: concluding with *prayer* and *praise*. (2 Sam. x.)

XXII. In this complaint and *prayer* of a persecuted sufferer the Psalmist is a type of Christ: (see 1 Pet. i. 11. Matth. xxvii. 46. John xix. 23); lamentation, comfort; lamentation again, comfort again; *prayer;* assurance of being heard: joy and *praise*, anticipation of the extension of God's kingdom: such is the subject-matter of this noble psalm.

XXIII. The Lord is the good shepherd of the believer. (2 Sam. xvii.)

XXIV. Probably sung at the entrance of the ark of the covenant to mount Zion. (2 Sam. vi. 1.) The Lord is God, Creator of the whole earth. Who shall dwell spiritually in His holy place? the truly righteous only. The ark drawing nigh, the gates of the tabernacle are commanded to open, and give entrance to the Lord of glory. Christ's ascension is typified.

XXV. David *prays* against foes and for pardon of sin. (2 Sam. xxiii.)

XXVI. David *prays* for help, on the ground of integrity and devotion to God's service: and resolves to *praise* the Lord for His mercies. (2 Sam. vi.)

XXVII. David's *prayer* of faith and confidence in God. (2 Sam. xviii.) Verse 12 is applicable to Christ. (Matth. xxvii. 59.)

XXVIII. A like *prayer* of faith in God, the Saviour of His Anointed and of His people. (2 Sam. vi.)

XXIX. The power and glory of God in a thunder-storm. (2 Sam. vi.)

XXX. David having been punished for the sin of pride (probably in numbering the people, 2 Sam. xxiv.), *praises* God for His deliverance. Sung at the dedication of the site of the future temple.

XXXI. David *prays* to God for help, relying on His justice: describes his own afflictions, and again prays: finally, assured of God's goodness to the righteous and to himself in particular, he exhorts all saints to *trust* in Him.

XXXII. The blessedness of pardoned sinners, a motive to penitence and uprightness. (2 Sam. xi.)

XXXIII. A *praise-psalm* to the Lord, true and faithful, righteous, merciful, and almighty, the sole guardian and redeemer of His saints.

XXXIV. A psalm of *praise*, in which the pious are invited to join, seeing that God will always help His people, as in the present instance. (2 Sam. xxiii.)

XXXV. A *prayer* against foes, whose cruelty and ingratitude are described (1 Sam. xxv.): ending with assurance and *praise*. Some verses are applicable to Messiah. (Joh. xv. 25. Matth. xxvii. 59.)

XXXVI. The wicked have no fear of God, but God's goodness prevails to defend the righteous: therefore David *prays* to Him against his foes. (1 Sam. xix.)

XXXVII. A psalm of *instruction*. Be not envious against evil-doers, who shall be cut off, while the righteous are protected. (2 Sam. xxiii.)

XXXVIII. A penitential *prayer* in affliction of body and soul. (2 Sam. xix.)

XXXIX. A *prayer-psalm*, written in sore distress and great commotion of spirit. From remonstrance, it proceeds to resignation, and ends with earnest intreaty. (2 Sam. xix.)

XL. The Psalmist, confirmed in faith by experience of God's mercies, declares the blessedness of trusting in God; *praises* God's glory; promises to show his gratitude by word and deed: in the second part, being still in great tribulation, he *prays* earnestly for deliverance. In Heb. x. this psalm is cited as applicable to Christ. (2 Sam. xxiii.)

XLI. The compassionate will receive compassion: on which ground David, in deep affliction and desertion, *prays* for support and deliverance. (2 Sam. xxiii.)

BOOK II.

XLII. XLIII. The Korahite psalmist, forsaken for a time by God, earnestly *prays* for renewed access to the sanctuary, and receives the assurance of faith. (2 Sam. xviii.)

XLIV. Complaint of oppressed Israel.

XLV. Nuptial song of *praise* to a king; typifying the union of Christ and His Church.

XLVI. The security of God's kingdom amidst the storms which shake the world.

XLVII. All people are summoned to *praise* God, who, after helping His people, has ascended His throne of glory. (2 Chron. xx.)

XLVIII. A song of *praise* to the great God, the Lord of Jerusalem, who defends Zion. (2 Chron. xx.)

XLIX. The prosperity of the wicked is but for a time.

L. The sacrifice of the heart alone well-pleasing to God.

LI. *Prayer* of the penitent David confessing his sin. (2 Sam. xi. xii.)

LII. Doom of the wicked, and triumph of the righteous: written by David against Doeg. (1 Sam. xxi.)

LIII. Nearly as XIV.

LIV. *Prayer* against persecutors (1 Sam. xxiii.), ending with confidence and praise.

LV. Earnest *prayer* against enemies and faithless friends, who are described: God will deliver those who *trust* in Him. (2 Sam. xv.)

LVI. David, sorely persecuted and menaced with death (1 Sam. xxi.), *prays* to God, and places full *trust* in Him.

LVII. David, *praying* to God in the cave (1 Sam. xxiv.), and assured of His protection against Saul, *praises* Him with rapture.

LVIII. David remonstrates with his persecutors, and *prays* against them to God, who will punish sinners and reward the just. (2 Sam. xv.)

LIX. *Prayer* of the innocent David when violently persecuted by Saul. (1 Sam. xix.)

LX. Written in celebration of the victory over Edom (2 Sam. viii. 13), and in prospect of an expedition against the land of Edom and Petra, its capital. The *prayer* of the people receives an answer from God, and, at the close, the king expresses his confidence that God will again give victory to his people.

LXI. The sorrowing king *prays* in *faith*.

LXII. The persecuted David rests on God alone and exhorts all men to do so, instead of relying on men and worldly goods. (2 Sam. xix.)

LXIII. God the *trusting* soul's only good.

LXIV. *Prayer* against the machinations of the wicked, whom God will certainly punish, and redress the righteous. (2 Sam. xvii.)

LXV. *Thanksgiving* to God for His manifold mercies, especially in giving rain and plenteous harvest.

LXVI. *Thanksgiving* of a grateful Church after trial.

LXVII. *Prayer* of the Church for God's grace.

LXVIII. A song of *thanksgiving* for victory, when the ark was brought back to Zion. God destroys the wicked, saves the righteous: has been the Saviour of Israel in her history. The procession is then described, and the conversion of the heathen prophesied. (2 Sam. xxiii.)

LXIX. A sufferer for the sake of God *prays* earnestly for deliverance, and, having the assurance of relief, *glorifies* God. Applied to Christ.

LXX. Extracted, with slight change, from Ps. XL, and prefatory to Ps. LXXI.

LXXI. *Prayer* of a sufferer, who, having experienced God's grace in his youth, desires its continuance in old age: and, being patient in tribulation, is also joyful in hope.

LXXII. Solomon and his righteous reign, typical of Christ and His kingdom of righteousness.

BOOK III.

LXXIII. Asaph, shocked by the prosperity of the wicked, describes the conflict of his mind, and the victory gained when he came to know that this prosperity is transient, and the future peace of the good certain: hence comes *faith* in God, and *praise* of His Name.

LXXIV. *Prayer* for oppressed and afflicted Israel. (1 Kings xxv.)

LXXV. The distressed people *praise* God, and rebuke their foes, relying on God, who will judge the world with power, and re-establish the tottering earth. (2 Kings xix.)

LXXVI. *Praise* of God who dwells in Zion, who has done great things for Israel, and controls the kings of earth. (2 Kings xix.)

LXXVII. The afflicted Israelite *prays* to God in anguish and doubt, but recovers *faith* and *trust*, remembering what great things God has done for His people.

LXXVIII. Asaph tells the story of Israel's sins, and his deliverances wrought by that God who has now chosen Zion for His sanctuary, and David for king.

LXXIX. Description of Jerusalem ruined by the Chaldæans, with *prayer* to God to deliver His people. (2 Kings xxiv.)
LXXX. *Prayer* to God to help His oppressed people, Joseph and Benjamin, who here represent Israel at large: Israel is described as God's vine, which the Lord is intreated to save.
LXXXI. Israel is exhorted to keep the Passover with joy, and to worship and *trust* the Lord, who has done such great things for His people: obedience would bring salvation.
LXXXII. God is made to remonstrate with the unjust judges of the earth, and intreated to rise Himself in judgment.
LXXXIII. *Prayer* against enemies addressed to God, who has hitherto defended Israel. (2 Chron. xx.)
LXXXIV. The Korahite (see Ps. xlii.) values the privileges of God's house, and *prays* for defence and blessing. (2 Sam. xviii.)
LXXXV. On the strength of ancient mercies, the people ' *pray* for deliverance, which in faith they anticipate from a gracious God.
LXXXVI. *Prayer* for deliverance on the ground of God's goodness, power, and past mercies. (2 Sam. xviii.)
LXXXVII. Jerusalem, the city of God, is loved and protected by Him: the heathen shall hereafter join it as their true home, and there find the fountains of Salvation. (2 Kings xx.)
LXXXVIII. Complaining *prayer* of one in the deepest misery. (2 Kings xxiv.)
LXXXIX. The Psalmist, with *joy and praise*, commemorates God's promises to David, and His preservation of Israel: paints the sad contrast of the existing time, and finally *prays* for new deliverance. (1 Kings xxiv.)

BOOK IV.

XC. Moses, seeing God's eternity and man's transience, *prays* for a wise heart and a blessing.

XCI. If God be for us, what shall be against us? Alternate language of *confidence* and exhortation.

XCII. The Psalmist resolves to *praise* God for His greatness and goodness in destroying the wicked and guarding the righteous.

XCIII. God mightier than the powers of the world.

XCIV. God is implored to avenge His people: the folly is shown of those who imagine that He does not see and hear and observe. He will save those who *trust* Him, and smite sinners.

XCV. Israel is invited to *praise* God, the Lord of the whole earth, and not to harden the heart like their fathers in the wilderness.

XCVI. Let the whole earth *praise* the Lord, who comes to judge it.

XCVII. The Lord comes to judgment in terrible majesty, shaming idolaters, gladdening Zion.

XCVIII. Glory from the whole earth to God the Redeemer and Judge.

XCIX. The Lord a King and Deliverer: such did faithful men of old find Him: His Name be *praised*.

C. A shout of *praise* and joy from earth to God.

CI. The Psalmist (David) resolves to *praise* God: and avows his determination to root out evil and promote good in his court and kingdom.

CII. The Psalmist, in the deepest affliction, flees to God, *praying* Him to restore Zion, and so achieve the conversion of the whole world: man is short-lived, God everlasting, and His servants shall abide with Him.

CIII. *Praise*, O my soul, the Lord, who is forgiving to thee, gracious to the opprest, and merciful to all men: man passes away, but God defends his people, and, as universal King, is to be praised by all creation.

CIV. The *praise* of God for His works in creation and providence: He will root out sinners.

CV. The judgments and wonders of God towards Israel in the past are the foundation of joyful hope for the future.

CVI. May God, rich in mercy to an obedient people, have compassion on His suffering Church: the sins of Israel have deserved and received chastisement: but now, as often before, God has heard their cry, and the Psalmist may *pray* to Him to complete their deliverance.

BOOK V.

CVII. *Praise* to God for His goodness in rescuing the Church from many troubles, with peculiar reference to the deliverance from Babylon.

CVIII. Borrowed partly from Ps. lvii. partly from Ps. lx.

CIX. The curse of the wicked, followed by the *prayer* of the oppressed and afflicted.

CX. A *prophecy* of the kingdom, priesthood, victories, sufferings, and exaltation of Messiah.

CXI. *Praise* to God for His great works and mercies shown to His people.

CXII. True righteousness and faith gain a *blessing* from God.

CXIII. The greatness and goodness of God, who dwelleth so high, yet regards with tender compassion the children of men.

CXIV. *Faith* encouraged by the remembrance of God's miraculous power, exerted for Israel of old.
CXV. *Prayer* for deliverance to the one true God, who is contrasted with heathen idols; with exhortation to Israel to trust and *praise* Him.
CXVI. The Psalmist blesses the Lord for deliverance from great trouble, and resolves to worship and *praise* Him in the sanctuary.
CXVII. All nations invited to *praise* the Lord: a conclusion to Psalm cxvi.
CXVIII. The Lord *praised* in the sanctuary for delivering His people. (Ezra iii. 10.) See Foot-note.
CXIX. A children's sermon in *praise* of God's Word, concluding the series of Psalms cvii...cxix.
CXX. The first of the Pilgrim Psalms. May the Lord, who delivered Israel of old, deliver him again from peace-hating slanderers.
CXXI. Heartfelt *trust* in God, the Keeper of Israel, sung in view of the mountains of Jerusalem.
CXXII. Glory of Jerusalem, and *prayers* for her salvation: sung at the city-gates, while arranging the procession to the sanctuary.
CXXIII. *Prayer* to God under distress and ill usage.
CXXIV. *Thanksgiving* to God the Protector of His Church.
CXXV. The faithful and true Israel is protected by God, but sinners are destroyed.
CXXVI. *Thanksgiving* for deliverance from Babylon.
CXXVII. All good is from God; dwelling, protection, food, children.
CXXVIII. Happy are they that fear God.
CXXIX. Israel, through much tribulation, has been delivered: may God still defeat his enemies.
CXXX. The distressed Church *prays* to God for deliverance and pardon; and waits, full of faith.
CXXXI. Humility of true faith.

CXXXII. Remembrance of David's zeal in building God's house, and of the divine grace and promise to him, as an encouragement to the work of temple-restoration in Israel.
CXXXIII. Brotherly love, when the people are assembled at Zion.
CXXXIV. *Praise* God, all His servants. Last of the Pilgrim Psalms.
CXXXV. This Psalm leads a group of twelve, sung at the dedication of the Second Temple. *Praise* God for His glory in nature and in grace to Israel: vain are heathen gods and their worshippers: praise God, all His servants.
CXXXVI. *Praise* to God as in Ps. cxxxv., with a burden: 'for His mercy endureth for ever.'
CXXXVII. The sorrow of Israel in Babylonia: punishment of Edom and Babylon: written after the capture of Babylon by Darius.
CXXXVIII. *Praise* to God for His promise of blessing to David.
CXXXIX. God, the all-seeing and all-knowing, *implored* to give His grace to the Psalmist, who is the enemy of all God's enemies.
CXL. *Prayer* of faith against wicked enemies.
CXLI. Evening *prayer*, in which David refers to events of his flight from Saul. (1 Sam. xxiv. xxvi. xxvii.)
CXLII. Complaint and earnest *supplication* to God.
CXLIII. Complaint, *supplication*, and hope.
CXLIV. David's *prayer* for himself and his people.
CXLV. Song of *praise* and *thanksgiving* from David and the Church.
CXLVI. *Praise-song* of Israel to the God of Zion.
CXLVII. First of a group of four Psalms, sung at the dedication of the city-walls under Nehemiah.

Praise to God for His great works, especially for the restoration of Jerusalem.

CXLVIII. All creatures invited to *praise* the Lord.

CXLIX. A new song of *thanks* for a great deliverance, in hope of future victory.

CL. A full-toned invitation to the *praise* of God.

INDEX II.

ADVICE to sinners: Psalms 4, 32, 62, 82, 95, 120.
Brotherly love: Psalm 133.
Christ typified:
    as King, Psalms 2, 45, 72, 110.
    as Bridegroom of the Church, Psalm 45.
    as a Conqueror, Psalms 2, 110, 118.
    as Priest, Psalm 110.
    as the true Vine, Psalm 80.
    as Son of Man, Psalms 8, 80.
    as an incarnate Saviour, Psalm 68.
    as Son of David, Psalm 132.
    in the character of David, Psalms 20, 21, 89, 101, 118, &c.
    as chief Cornerstone, Psalm 118.
    as an obedient Son, Psalm 40.
    as Prophet of the Church, Psalms 22, 40.
    as Sufferer, Psalms 16, 22, 69, 89.
    as rejected by sinners, Psalms 2, 110, 118.
    as defeating death and the grave, Psalms 16, 49.
    as having ascended to glory, Psalms 24, 47, 68.
    as Lord of all and Prince of peace, Psalms 2, 72, 85.

Church of Christ typified:
    as Bride of Christ, Psalm 45.
    as Jerusalem or Israel, Psalms 48, 80, 87, 122, 129, 132, 133, 135, &c.
    in her final triumph and glory, Psalms 87, 97, 102.

Faith:
    expressed, Psalms 11, 13, 16, 17, 25, 27, 28, 42, 43, 46, 52, 55, 56, 62, 63, 69, 71, 73, 81, 86, 94, 116, 142, 143.
    its blessing, Psalms 2, 33, 50, 91, 125, 131.

GOD: (Elohim, or God in general: Jehovah, or Lord, as God of Israel.)
    His eternity, Psalms 90, 92, 93, 102, 119.
    His power, greatness and glory, Psalms 2, 8, 11, 18, 19, 22, 24, 29, 33, 40, 46, 47, 48, 60, 65, 68, 74, 76, 77, 86, 89, 97, 98, 99, 102, 104, 108, 113, 115, 118, 139, 145.
    His works of creation and providence, Psalms 8, 33, 65, 104, 136, 146, 147, 148.
    His wisdom and knowledge, Psalms 9, 10, 11, 33, 66, 73, 92, 94, 119, 136, 139, 147.
    His benevolence, Psalms 36, 65, 71, 104, 107, 136, 145, 146, 147.
    His mercy, Psalms 25, 30, 32, 36, 46, 57, 62, 65, 68, 71, 73, 86, 89, 100, 102, 103, 107, 108, 113, 116, 118, 130, 136, 138.
    His care for those who trust in Him, Psalms 3, 4, 5, 9, 10, 11, 14, 16, 18, 23, 25, 27, 29, 31, 34, 37, 41, 44, 46, 48, 53, 55, 59, 60, 64, 66, 68, 69, 70, 73, 77, 80, 90, 91, 92, 94, 95, 97, 98, 99, 102, 103, 108, 109, 111, 113, 115, 119, 121, 124, 127, 140, 145, 148, 149.
    His holiness and abhorrence of sin, Psalms 5, 11, 14, 25, 34, 36, 37, 50, 51, 52, 53, 64, 68, 69, 73, 92, 99, 109, 119, 140.
    His justice and truth, Psalms 7, 9, 10, 36, 50, 58, 62,

65, 67, 68, 73, 75, 76, 86, 89, 94, 96, 98, 99, 111, 138, 146.

Heathen :—
    humbled, Psalms 9, 33, 46, 47, 68, 78, 135, 136.
    reproved, Psalms 115, 135.
    converted to God, Psalms 22, 51, 68, 87.

Humility :—
    Psalms 22, 39, 131.

Israel :—
    defended by the Lord, Psalms 44, 68, 69, 76, 78, 81, 85, 89, 103, 105, 106, 114, 115, 126, 129, 131, 135, 147, 148.
    afflicted, Psalms 44, 74, 78, 79, 80, 85, 102, 129.
    prayed for, Psalms 14, 53, 59, 60, 85, 102, 144.
    events in the history of, Psalms 44, 68, 69, 72, 74, 77, 78, 80, 81, 83, 105, 106, 114, 126, 132, 135, 136, 137.

Man :—
    His greatness, Psalm 8.
    His weakness and transience, Psalms 39, 49, 62, 90, 102, 103, 146.

Prayer :—
    for help against enemies, Psalms 3, 7, 9, 10, 12, 13, 17, 25, 28, 31, 35, 38, 40, 41, 42, 43, 54, 55, 56, 58, 59, 60, 64, 69, 70, 71, 74, 79, 82, 83, 94, 109, 115, 139, 140, 141, 142, 144.
    for grace and protection, Psalms 4, 13, 16, 25, 28, 31, 36, 42, 43, 44, 57, 60, 61, 62, 67, 80, 84, 86, 106, 108, 118, 119, 123, 138.
    for guidance and instruction, Psalms 5, 12, 26, 71, 90, 119, 139.
    for pardon, Psalms 39, 51, 60, 130.
    in affliction, Psalms 6, 10, 12, 13, 22, 31, 35, 38, 39, 40, 42, 43, 60, 69, 77, 79, 80, 86, 88, 102, 109, 130, 142, 143.
    penitential, Psalms 6, 32, 38, 51, 102, 130, 143.
    of a soul longing for God, Psalms 42, 43, 63, 143.

at morning, Psalms 3, 5.
at evening, Psalms 4, 63, 141.
for prince and people, Psalms 18, 20, 89, 144.

Public Worship:—
Psalms 5, 26, 27, 84, 118, 122.

Righteousness:—
its description, Psalms 1, 15, 17, 36, 112, 128.
its blessedness, Psalms 1, 5, 11, 15, 16, 18, 24, 37, 40, 41, 111, 112, 128.

Sin:—
its description, Psalms 1, 5, 10, 14, 36, 37, 52, 53, 55, 58, 64, 73.
its evil fate, Psalms 1, 5, 7, 9, 10, 14, 21, 37, 52, 53, 59, 69, 73, 104, 109, 112, 125, 129, 140.

Sovereign:—
prayed for, Psalms 20, 61, 72, 134.
relies on God, Psalms 21, 63, 101, 144.
blest by God, Psalms 89, 118, 132.
his righteous resolutions, Psalm 101.

Thanksgiving and Praise:—
general, Psalms 8, 33, 47, 65, 66, 67, 68, 72, 75, 81, 89, 92, 95, 96, 98, 100, 103, 104, 105, 106, 108, 111, 113, 115, 117, 118, 134, 135, 136, 138, 145, 146, 147, 148, 149, 150.
for hearing of prayer, Psalms 7, 22, 28, 66.
for deliverance, Psalms 9, 17, 18, 30, 31, 32, 35, 40, 54, 56, 69, 71, 89, 103, 107, 109, 116, 118.
for protection and grace, Psalms 16, 18, 28, 31, 34, 40, 44, 47, 57, 68, 71, 107, 144.
for instruction, Psalms 16, 71.

Word of God:—
its excellence, Psalms 12, 19, 33, 119, 138.

THE END.

www.ingramcontent.com/pod-product-compliance
Lightning Source LLC
Chambersburg PA
CBHW032104230426
43672CB00009B/1632